"Don't Quote Me"

An Inspiring and Honest Approach to
Discovering a Healthier and Happier Life

Steven Pollack

BALBOA.
PRESS
A DIVISION OF HAY HOUSE

Balboa Press books may be ordered through booksellers or by contacting:

Balboa Press
A Division of Hay House
1663 Liberty Drive
Bloomington, IN 47403
www.balboapress.com
1 (877) 407-4847

Print information available on the last page.

ISBN: 978-1-4525-5544-7 (sc)
ISBN: 978-1-4525-5545-4 (hc)
ISBN: 978-1-4525-5738-0 (e)

Library of Congress Control Number: 2012915225

Balboa Press rev. date: 01/26/2017

Dedications

To my wife, Stacy, for putting up with me and taking care of me for the past thirty-five years and for inspiring me to become the person I am today.

To my unbelievable kids, Alexa and Michael, for putting up with my "in life" speeches and giving me the tools and experiences to learn and grow from. You have inspired me through your own achievements to set the bar even higher for myself.

Special thanks to my friends for putting up with my competitive but loving nature; Salty for asking the question, "Why don't you write a book?"; my brother Mark for telling me to publish it; DK for allowing me to read it to you; the thousands of inspiring people whom I have observed, learned from, and quoted in my book; and all the people who will read this book and hopefully gain some insight into their own abilities to improve their own lives through the inspiration of others.

Lastly, I dedicate this book to Nan and Gramps for showing me all the unconditional love anyone could hope for and teaching me an appreciation for life in the process.

Introduction

I AM WRITING THIS BOOK because as I have gotten older, I have noticed things that seem so obvious to me now that didn't before. I figured that someone could benefit from my experiences and reality checks in a world filled with confusion. I'm not saying that I'm smarter than you or better looking or more successful. I am no more an expert than anyone else, but I have definite opinions that make a lot of sense to me, and I think some of them will make sense to you. This is a collection of observations, experiences, and advice mixed in with inspirational quotes and a sense of humor. If you don't have a sense of humor or are not looking to be inspired and haven't bent the first page, you could try returning it.

You bent the first page, didn't you? Oh, well then, what have you got to lose? It's a New York mentality, been there, done that" school of thought. It was less about writing a book and more about sharing my perspective. The purpose was not to provide a blueprint. I've grown tired of all the fad diets, misinformation, irresponsible reporting, political rhetoric, and downright bullshit! Somewhat inspired by the "Just Say No" campaign aimed at drugs, which was started by First Lady Nancy Reagan. I like that bottom line, black-or-white approach—enough with the excuses and reasoning. Just say no. You could finish this book on a shuttle flight before you land—or in the bathroom (one good colonoscopy prep should get you through). It's more of an inspirational handbook. I tried to take Bono's advice and write as if I were dead. Seems like a more honest approach and the best way to write without compromise. Personally, I have always found inspiration from the poetry of classic rock-and-roll lyrics (fewer artists inspire me today), and I've tried to share some of my favorites, as well as other inspirational quotes from a variety of sources.

> **"Call me a relic, call me what you will / Say I'm old fashion, say I'm over the hill. / Today's music ain't got the same soul / I like that old time rock and roll."**
> **—Bob Seger, "Old Time Rock and Roll"**

My hope is that this book inspires some of you to understand that *you* have the power to change the way *you* live your life—to understand that it's within all of us to make the choices that dictate our lives. All aspects of your life are a reflection of the choices you make. If you want a different result, then you have to make a different choice.

> **"Life is a sum of all your choices."**
> **—Albert Camus, Nobel Prize–winning journalist**

A healthy and balanced approach to diet/fitness, work routine, and family life is all up to the choices you make. Self-discipline, moderation, and logic are the keys to a balanced lifestyle. The only tools that you will need are initiative and the will to succeed. If some of the content seems cliché and obvious, that's because it is. This is not rocket science! Simplification, instead of complication, is easier to achieve than you think. I urge you not to skim or speed-read this book, as you might miss the intended context or the true meaning behind a great quote.

I must confess that I have never read a "self-help" book and don't care much for the term (sounds too desperate and negative). I prefer to think of this book as a positive-thinking, inspirational avenue to "self-awareness." *Awareness* implies knowledge gained through one's own perceptions or by means of information. Once you're aware that the answers are within all of us, you will hopefully gain the insight and self-confidence to attain a sustainable healthy and balanced lifestyle. Life is a journey as well as a process. It may take you some time to realize that the power has always been within. Just as Dorothy from "The Wizard of Oz", discovered that she always had the power to return home to Kansas. And, NO, clicking your heels together three times will not apply here. Just know that none of us is perfect, and perfection is not the goal of this book. Nothing I speak of in this book is meant for drastic change. I don't have, nor can I give you, all the answers. Besides, think of how boring it would be to know it all. The best teacher in life is experience. I'm not telling you right from wrong (we all have a moral compass) or how to live your life. I will leave that up to the self-proclaimed "self-help" experts. This book is merely a collection of observations and information sprinkled with some honest and logical advice from me and other far more intelligent and inspiring people. The goal here is to inspire the self-confidence that will allow you to discover your own individual formula for a successful, happy life.

Quotes

WHEN LIFE GETS TOUGH, AND rest assured it will—I don't care what tax bracket you're in—there are four quotes that have always helped me through. We all go through periods of difficulty when we feel like life is out to get us no matter how hard we try. When I'm feeling sorry for myself and want to give up, I remember the quote that Jimmy Valvano (North Carolina State basketball coach) gave at the ESPY awards in March 1993 upon accepting the Arthur Ashe Courage Award when he knew he was dying of a rare cancer. He knew it would be the last time he saw most of the audience (many of whom were his friends). In one of the most riveting and inspirational speeches I can remember, he said,

"Don't give up. ... Don't ever give up!"

That is now the motto of the Jimmy V Foundation.

It's bottom line simplicity; nothing more needs to be said. If you throw it in, you're done. If you are lucky enough to wake up and draw a breath, then it's a good day and you have the right to choose how you live it!

"No matter how you feel, get up, dress up, show up, and never give up!"
—Unknown

Jimmy V spoke of having an enthusiasm for life and having a dream or a goal—this bit of optimism and wisdom from a dying man. If a dream were easy to achieve, it wouldn't be a dream. You just have to pick your dreams and focus on a direction.

> **"If you follow every dream, you might get lost."**
> **—Neil Young, "The Painter"**

Everything in life worth a damn is worth fighting for. Persistence and determination will pave the way to success.

> **"Sheer persistence is the difference between success and failure."**
> **—Donald Trump**

You simply have to believe in yourself and your dream, and you better be willing to fight for it!

> **"The future belongs to those who believe in their dreams."**
> **—Eleanor Roosevelt**

Nothing in life is free—nothing! I'm not saying that some days are not better than others, but "Don't give up, don't ever give up." I urge you to download the whole speech from the Internet. He says, "There are three things we all should do every day. We should do this every day of our lives. Number one is laugh. You should laugh every day. Number two is think. You should spend some time in thought. Number three is, you should have your emotions moved to tears, could be happiness or joy. But think about it. If you laugh, you think, and you cry, that's a full day. That's a heck of a day. You do that seven days a week, you're going to have something special."

He concludes his speech by saying, "Cancer can take away all my physical ability. It cannot touch my mind; it cannot touch my heart; and it cannot touch my soul. And those three things are going to carry on forever." Wow, I get a chill every time I read it. (Come on, admit it. You got a chill.) Seeing it live was powerful and inspirational.

"Don't count the days, make the days count."
—Muhammad Ali

Stuart Scott, the groundbreaking ESPN anchor who recently died of a rare cancer at the age of forty-nine, upon accepting the Jimmy V Perseverance Award at the ESPYs, penned an equally inspirational and moving speech six months before he passed away, echoing Jimmy V's words about not giving up.

In a powerful, heartfelt moment, he said, "Cancer is not about surviving, but how people live their lives. When you die, that does not mean you lose to cancer. You beat cancer by how you live and in the manner in which you live. So live. Live. Fight like hell. And when you get too tired to fight, then lay down and rest and let somebody else fight for you. That's also very, very important. I can't do this 'don't give up' thing all by myself."

His companion, Kristen Spodobalski, told him that "life consisted of two dates with a dash in between." Scott's moving closing words were these: "I hope my infant girls take this with them: *make the dash count*."

The other quote that I have turned to for inspiration is from my favorite poet/artist/storyteller, Bruce Springsteen. It's from the album *Darkness on the Edge of Town* in a song called "Badlands":

"Well, keep pushin' till it's understood and these badlands start treating us good."

It was actually the quote that we had on our high school soccer T-shirts, and it stuck with me. It's easier to make excuses or to give up or settle. Perseverance takes commitment! When you think you can't dig any deeper, keep digging. "Keep pushin' till it's understood and these badlands start treating *you* good." They will, eventually. Age and time teaches wisdom, and you learn that life is a marathon, not a sprint. Pace yourself; keep the highs in check, and manage the lows. Take a chance and take control of your life.

"You miss 100 percent of the shots you don't take."
—Wayne Gretzky, hockey player

Take a calculated risk. My son was recently at a Q & A with Billy Joel at college and had the guts to ask if they could play together. Billy said yes, and the video went viral (30 million views in all). Soon after, he appeared on the *Today show, Good Day New York, CNN, Sirius radio, and The Jeff Probst Show.*

"Great moments are born from great opportunity."
—Herb Brooks, 1980 USA Olympic hockey gold-medal coach

He was asked to write a song about his experience and perform it on national TV. It's about being alive and taking a risk. He had to write it in a week. It has since been featured on Sirius radio. Here is the chorus:

"You may be alive but are you living? I promise you the two are not the same. Never hesitate to

**take what's given. Cause chances are this chance
won't come again."
—Michael Pollack, "Chances Are"**

Do something that you have talked about forever—run that marathon, commit to getting in shape, finish your education, or save for that lifelong dream vacation and take it. Buy that Harley and just ride! Don't talk yourself out of it and decide to put the money in another safe mutual fund for the future. (For me, it's writing this book.) Forget the conventional "Bucket List", and put together a "F**k-it List", instead. Challenge yourself to do things that make you less comfortable. The future is now; the time is now.

**"Life is not measured by the number of breaths
we take but by the moments that take our breath
away."
—George Carlin**

You only live once, and believe me, you will be a better parent, partner, and person if you are a happy one. My new mantra is "SOLO": Steven Only Lives Once! That doesn't mean don't plan for the future or make prudent, responsible investments. Nothing I say is meant for drastic change. It's all about moderation!

The third quote came much later in life, with perspective.

**"The road to happiness lies in two simple
principles. Find what it is that interests you
and that you can do well, and put your whole
heart and soul into it, every bit of energy and
ambition and natural ability that you have."
—John D. Rockefeller III**

After working for years and actually doing something that I was good at and enjoyed at times, this became clearer. Life can be a grind.

> **"Your gift is the thing you do *best* with the *least* amount of effort."**
> **—Steve Harvey, comedian and talk show host**

Both my kids are fortunate to have a real passion for something. Being able to incorporate that love into your everyday routine can be extremely rewarding.

> **"If you follow your passion, you will eventually find your purpose."**
> **—Steve Harvey**

You won't actually realize or understand this until you are forty or fifty and resent the everyday grind of life. Choose a job you love, and you will never have to work a day in your life.

> **"If you are working on something exciting that you really care about, you don't have to be pushed. The vision pulls you."**
> **—Steve Jobs, Apple cofounder**

Life is a challenge. However, if you incorporate a passion, it can be much more rewarding, although not always easy! The fourth and one of my favorite quotes of all time is another quote I heard from Steve Harvey, who was quoting Mark Twain:

> **"The two most important days in your life are the day you are born and the day you find out why."**

Parenting

LET'S START THIS SECTION OFF with a quote, just to give you perspective.

"Raising a child is the only relationship you have where if you do it right, it will end in separation." —Naomi Foner, mother of actors Jake and Maggie Gyllenhaal

I am lucky to have two healthy (and that, my friends, is all that counts), terrific kids, and I do believe that my wife and I had something to do with it. It sounds cocky, but I have always said that you can put twenty families in a room and probably tell me which kid belongs to which parent just by spending some time with everyone—and it's not just genetics. Your kids are the product of your beliefs and lifestyle. They possess similar characteristics, idiosyncrasies, and mannerisms, as well as confidence, drive, and desire. The apple truly does not fall far from the tree. Your actions do speak louder than your words.

I have always believed in honesty with my kids, to a point. Too much unnecessary information is not always the best idea. For instance, plead guilty to a lesser offense. Telling your kids that you tried pot makes sense to me at the right age. They won't respect you if they know you are lying (as long as you let them know that you didn't inhale—or was it exhale?). But telling them that you attended Woodstock on Quaaludes and LSD and made love to a stranger while Janus Joplin sang "Me and Bobby McGee" is too much information. You get the idea.

Be an active part of their lives. Embrace your children's passions and accept who they are, not who you want them to be.

**"Raise the child you got—not the one you want."
—Nancy Rose, author**

Share in their interests, not just yours. And most of all, listen. By listening, I mean not multitasking but making eye contact and engaging them. (They know the difference even at very early ages.)

I have coached my kids and their friends from kindergarten until they went to middle school and have always tried to make it fun and competitive at the same time. I know that some people profess that youth sports shouldn't be competitive, just fun for all. News flash: sports and life are competitive! Get used to it. I have learned more of what I apply in life from being part of competitive teams and have always believed that sports are a metaphor for life. You can find out a lot about yourself and others by competing in sports.

**"Sports do not build character. They reveal it."
—John Wooden, UCLA basketball coach**

You learn how to coexist and depend on others and how to get more accomplished as part of a team than as an individual. Magic Johnson reworked a famous quote from John F. Kennedy when he said,

"Ask not what your teammates can do for you.
Ask what you can do for your teammates."

Like they (Who are they? Any ideas?) say, there is no *I* in team! More *we* and less *me*. Being competitive doesn't mean playing the better kids longer at an early age. Personally, I have always felt much more rewarded when a kid of lesser skill does something great, bringing a smile to his or her face and to mine—a kid who will probably not pursue sports but had a positive experience rather than a negative one. We have all witnessed these crazy father/coaches who damage a kid's ego and confidence forever. Don't think for a minute that those experiences don't leave a lasting impression. I still remember the worst coach I ever had, and I'm sure many of you had a similar experience. Usually those are the dads who never had athletic success when they were young and are living vicariously through their kids.

Loud encouragement is great; just make sure you are yelling *for* a kid and not *at* a kid. You can teach a child more by being constructive rather than destructive. If kids feel overwhelmed, they will likely tune you out before you can get your point across. I played a lot of competitive sports growing up and would rather impart my experience and love for the game. Wow, I am making myself sound like a saint. News flash: I'm not! I just have a bottom line mentality, and as I have gotten older, I've become less tolerant of obvious bullshit!

"I am not a saint, unless you think of a saint as a
sinner who keeps on trying."
—Nelson Mandela

What's with parents trying to be best friends with their kids? Kids don't need you to be their best friend. They need limits. They will appreciate you more for it in the end. Don't coddle them; teach them independence, resiliency, and respect at an early age. Empower them to be curious and confident. Encourage them to visualize and imagine. A vivid imagination can increase performance and potentially alter an outcome.

> **"The world of reality has its limits; the world of imagination is boundless."**
> **—Jean Jacques Rousseau, composer**

Use the power of your imagination to visualize vividly what you would like to be successful in.

> **"The best way to predict the future is to invent it."**
> **—Alan Kay, scientist**

Bob Bowmen, the coach of Olympic swimmer Michael Phelps says that "Phelps is the best that he has ever seen in terms of athletes visualizing their race outcomes. Phelps has the amazing ability to visualize or imagine the perfect race as if he is sitting in the stands and as if he is in the water.

> **"Your imagination is your preview of life's coming attractions."**
> **—Albert Einstein**

If you harness the infinite power of your imagination and dream bigger, the possibilities are endless.

> **"The power of imagination makes us infinite."**
> **—John Muir, author**

Show your kids a lot of love and affection. The only advice I ever gave to my kids was, "Don't kill yourself!". If you are a great kid and get in a car with someone you believe to be compromised, then you are no longer in control of your outcome. My kids have always called my wife and I, no matter the situation, and they've had the confidence that we would never question them in the moment but always hold them accountable the next day. We would discuss the situation and listen to the circumstances because not everything is black and white. I love that not only our kids had the confidence to call us in a crisis, but so many of their friends, did as well. My wife and I work, and it's been my observation that the children of two working parents seem more comfortable in their own skin, better adjusted and more independent than those overly coddled by stay-at-home moms. I'm not saying there's anything wrong with staying at home, Mom. Just give your kid a little space. Trust me; the space is just as necessary for you.

> **"Good parents give their children Roots and Wings. Roots to know where home is, wings to fly away and exercise what's been taught them."**
> **—Jonas Salk**

Being a kid today is hard enough, and the world waits for no one. Growing up in the new millennium seems more complex than ever. More choices and options in a fast-changing technological world can be challenging, at best.

> **"Into this house we're born, into this world we're thrown."**
> **—The Doors, "Riders on the Storm"**

That said, many kids today believe they are entitled to something. They think the world owes them a break. Judge Phillip B. Gilliam of Denver, Colorado, who regularly dealt with youth, offered the following words in 1959, and those same words still ring true today. "Always we hear the cry from teenagers. What can we do, where can we go?" His answer is this:

> "Go home, mow the lawn, wash the windows, learn to cook, build a raft, get a job, visit the sick, study your lessons and after you've finished, read a book. Your town does not owe you recreational facilities and your parents do not owe you fun. The world does not owe you a living, you owe the world something. You owe it your time, energy and talent so that no one will be at war, in sickness and lonely again. In other words grow up, stop being a cry baby, get out of your dream world and develop a backbone not a wishbone. Start behaving like a responsible person. You are important and you are needed. It's too late to sit around and wait for somebody to do something someday. Someday is now and that somebody is you!"

Now, that's tough love!

> **"Someday is not a day of the week."**
> **—Denise Brennan Nelson, author**

Encouragement and support go a long way to developing a child's confidence. If you make kids, feel like there's nothing they can't accomplish, they just might believe you. They have no other point of reference or experience with failure to know the difference. Helping them to create a strong self-image will lay the foundation for a successful outcome. Leading by example is the best form of encouragement. If you show them that anything is possible, they already have the proof. If they see you give up, the tone has been set. Show them that good can come from failure and that you only really fail when you don't even try. There's nothing wrong with falling down; just make sure you fall forward. Teach them the importance of learning from their mistakes and failures. As J. K. Rowling (author of the Harry Potter books) said in a 2008 commencement address at Harvard University:

> **"It is impossible to live without failing at something, unless you live so cautiously that you might as well not have lived at all—in which case, you fail by default."**

Many amateur golfers will knock a putt six feet past the hole for a birdie and hang their head in disgust, while the pro will watch the ball as it rolls past the hole to see just how the ball breaks, making it easy to putt it in for par. Don't be afraid to admit that you're wrong, and be willing to apologize. Let your kids be comfortable that you are not perfect, and they don't have to be either. Encouraging them to take a chance to fail will eventually enable them to succeed.

> **"Every father should remember that one day his son will follow his example instead of his advice."**
> **—Charles F. Kettering, American inventor**

So practice what you preach!

It's also been my observation that kids today have way too many activities and "playdates." Social activity is great, but it's equally as important for children to have downtime and to learn how to occupy themselves. We all need relaxation time and a safe haven where we can wind down. It's important to fill your home with love and cherished memories of time spent together. For example, in our home, pictures of time spent as a family and memorable trinkets from vacations help remind us of happy times. An expensive home filled with pricey, hollow furnishings that are void of character and memories is not warm and welcoming to me.

> **"I've still got to let you know, a house still doesn't make a home."**
> **—U2, "Sometimes You Can't Make It on Your Own"**

It's what's inside those four walls that make the difference. A home is a place where life happens. A word of advice: spend as much quality time with your kids as possible. Buying them lavish presents doesn't make up for being away.

> **"Children need your presence more than your presents."**
> **—Jesse Jackson**

If your work happens to keep you away, that's fine; just make the most of the moments you do have together and find other ways to make your children feel connected to your life. I heard Matt Lauer say:

> **"We are defined as parents by who we are from five to nine, not nine to five."**

In today's technological age with e-mail, instant/text messaging, video computers, cell phones, etc., you have no excuses. That said, try not to let technology prevail and set limits. We have become an engrossed, head-down, mobile device society of people crashing into one another. Try putting yourself on a "digital diet", and spend more quality time with your kids. Putting gadgets away during family time is a simple way of creating technology boundaries. Engage in life instead of technology. Social media is great, but a little less media and a bit more social can benefit all. Don't let the time slip by, and be sure to take lots of pictures and video.

"I'm just an analog guy living in a digital world."
—Hank Moody, *Californication*

I am the resident videographer in my family (fewer video cameras these days), which means you will rarely see me in the video. I am like the narrative voice from the 1980s TV show *The Wonder Years*. I don't know about you, but no matter how much I charge the stupid camera battery, every time I use it I get that blinking light, letting me know that I have precious few minutes to capture whatever important occasion. My family's life is relegated to a short story filled with small clips of important moments. Kidding aside, pictures and video are as important for you as they are for your children, and with today's digital video/camera phones, no excuses! You really do wake up one day and poof, they're gone.

There's a great children's book written by Jamie Lee Curtis called *Is There Really a Human Race?* It's a book about relishing the journey of life rather than rushing it away and making good choices along the way. The book was inspired by the question asked by Jamie Lee's youngest son. We all seem to be in a great rush. What are we rushing away besides life itself?

"Many of us spend half of our time wishing for things we could have if we didn't spend half our time wishing."
—Alexander Woollcott, American critic

Strap yourself in and enjoy the ride. Count on it being complicated, unpredictable, and irrational—it's all part of the journey, and over time we begin to realize that "the journey" is the destination." Parenting exposes a range of emotions—profound, painful, intense, and rewarding. Sometimes all at once. Don't wish any stage of development away, and know that the next stage is just as great as the one before. Okay, except for some of those teen years. (I need to keep it honest.)

My daughter came down for breakfast one day at about the age of thirteen and started to speak. I thought to myself, *who are you? What have you done with my daughter?* Be true to your values and don't give in, thinking you will lose your child. Hold strong on the important issues (no matter how difficult), but let your children know that you are listening as well. Be willing to make concessions when appropriate. It's important for the growth and evolution of your relationship with your kids for them to know that you are sensitive to their situations and needs. Don't underestimate the social and peer pressures that these kids face in their teen years. There are a lot of tricky elements in the new world. Kids eventually come full circle, and the relationship grows stronger. Mind you, my kids recently graduated from college, so it's perfectly fine for you more experienced parents to laugh out loud at me. Kind of like, "Poor schmuck has no idea what he's about to face."

"Listening"

I own an executive search (headhunting) firm in New York City, and when I started out, I would talk so fast there were actually times I didn't even understand what I was saying. I remember a time early on in my career when I was closing a deal with a candidate to accept a position with my client. I started to go off a hundred miles a minute until finally the person stopped me and said, "Steven, I didn't understand a word you just said." I was like, *Wow! She's right!* That day I stopped talking (well, not completely) and started listening. Guess what? People have a lot to say, and if you actually listen, you might even learn something. Lean in! I have been learning ever since. Speaking slower does not mean thinking slower. There is a reason that the ear is shaped like a question mark—listen more and broadcast less.

> **"Learn to listen. Opportunity sometimes knocks very softly."**
> **—H. Jackson Brown Jr., author**

Listening has become a lost art, especially with the elderly. We are a society that shuns the elderly and puts them out to pasture. News flash: that's our future as well. Sooner or later you play all the parts. A lot can be learned from someone who has lived a lifetime of lessons. Mistakes can be learned from and even benefited from. A lot has been accomplished before you were even born. French playwright Jean Racine speaks of the old valuing their wrinkles as "the imprints of exploits," clear evidence of a life lived to its fullest.

If you are fortunate enough to have grandparents or important relationships with elderly people, don't be afraid to ask them some important questions. Learning of any loved one's experience and knowledge over a lifetime is a gift and will provide a roadmap for your own journey. Jody Gastfield, VP of senior care services at Health.com, encourages people fortunate to have a parent or grandparent to ask the following six questions:

1. What have you enjoyed most about aging?
2. What are the biggest challenges of growing old?
3. What has surprised you the most in your years?
4. What has brought you the most joy?
5. What would you do differently?
6. What words of advice do you have for my generation, as we try to grow closer to—and guide—our children?

The problem with the new generation is that they think they know it all and anything previous is antiquated. They are not yet aware of the big picture. The landscape will always change, but *life* does not! I try to take a little something from those around me. It could be a recipe for the grill or something that helps me become a better parent, husband, lover, or whatever. Don't be so arrogant as to think that you can't learn from others, even if you don't think they are as smart as you. News flash: you're not as smart as you think!

> **"It's what you learn after you know it all that counts."**
> **—John Wooden, UCLA basketball coach**

I have a friend (an ex-neighbor) who has had her ups and downs. One day, after seeing me grinding every day (climbing the ladder, working hard to get to the next level, etc.), she asked, "Why don't you take a break for a minute and appreciate what you have achieved so far?" I looked at her like, *What?* Guess what? She was right. We are all so caught up in trying to succeed and advance that sometimes we simply have to "stop and smell the roses." It sounds cliché, but try it. You won't be sorry. People today tend to plan their lives out so far in advance that they lose focus on the present.

> **"Life is what happens when you're busy making other plans."**
> **—John Lennon, "Beautiful Boy"**

We seem to base success on accomplishments that shape our inevitable legacy. I do think it's important to work hard and have goals, but it's no less important to take a step back every now and again. There's a great line from a Jim Croce song called "One Less Set of Footsteps":

> **"After all, it's what we've done that makes us what we are."**

We all strive so hard, but as a culture, we never seem satisfied. To quote another line in the Springsteen song "Badlands":

> **"Poor men wanna be rich, rich men wanna be Kings, and a King ain't satisfied till he rules everything."**

We all want what we don't have, and we are a society of envy. Envy can be the source of much unhappiness. Forget keeping up with the Joneses (and who are they anyway?). You say you're happy for your friend who just got a big promotion or inheritance, but are you really?

> **"A true friend is one who overlooks your failures and tolerates your success!"**
> **—Doug Larson, cartoonist**

It's not that you don't wish good things for your friends, but let's be honest. What you're really thinking is, *Why him and not me?*

> **"The only true currency in this bankrupt world is what you share with someone else when you're uncool."**
> **—Lester Bangs, *Almost Famous***

Honesty can be quite liberating. Just be honest, and don't forget to listen!

"Dependency and Denial"

WE ARE A SOCIETY OF dependencies—drugs, alcohol, therapy, chiropractic, reality TV, or whatever. Dependency can be defined as the state of being determined, influenced, or controlled by something else.

> **"Rehab is for quitters!"**
> **—Hank Moody, *Californication***

> **"There is no dependence that can be sure but a dependence upon one's self."**
> **—John Gay, English poet**

Be responsible. Don't drink and drive—it's not a formula for success. That doesn't mean don't drink, just have someone drive you home. Oh, and by the way, drinking too much is also not a potential formula for success. Just ask the people who were with you that night. It sounds something like this: "I did that? Oh shit!" Take two aspirin, drink a lot of water, and when you feel better, you will conveniently forget that feeling and do it all over again. It's just another example of how we lie to ourselves.

> **"Warning: The consumption of alcohol may lead you to think people are laughing with you."**
> **—W. C. Fields**

The human spirit has a unique quality that serves as a convenient mechanism for self-reinforcement: it's called denial! We tend to conveniently alter the truth to satisfy our subconscious. We are all too aware that we are misleading ourselves but seem to disregard the reality and categorically deny the obvious truth. Don't underestimate the power. It's like a get-out-of-jail-free card. We are lying to ourselves and actually believe our ridiculous indiscretions as absolutely right. Let's be clear: denial is not good! You and I know that, but it serves as a protective layer that can't be questioned until you screw up again. Oh, and you will; it's just a matter of when. The best thing to do is have a face-to-face conversation with yourself—come on now, I talk to myself all the time, and I'm hoping you do as well. Denial can only deepen and get more perplexing, as is the case with any lie. It starts small and grows fast. Be honest with yourself, or you will surely be in trouble.

> **"Most men would rather deny a hard truth than face it."**
> **—George R.R. Martin, author, *A Game of Thrones***

If you need to handle an issue on your own, it's all good, but when it gets past self-help, reach out in confidence to someone who will support you the right way but make you deal either way.

> **"The best way out is through."**
> **—Robert Frost, poet**

Some things can be managed with willpower and the fear of losing everything; others cannot. We all think we are in total control until that day when we do something that we thought we never would and can't fathom why. Go to a trusting source for help and accept tough love. It's better to face your demons head-on. The other option is addiction and is far more complex.

> **"Time decides who you meet in life, your heart decides who you want in your life, and your behavior decides who stays in your life."**
> **—Unknown**

We all like to tell ourselves convenient lies that we start to believe. It's like moving a golf ball when you're playing alone or conveniently not taking a stroke penalty. Who are you lying to? After a while, we start to believe our own lies and can't decipher them from the truth. I confess—I have moved my golf ball.

> **"Golf is a game in which you yell 'fore,' shoot six, and write down five."**
> **—Paul Harvey, journalist**

Okay, I still move my golf ball! But I am growing from the experience. LOL. For those of you who don't have kids on the Internet, *LOL* means "laughing out loud." That's a whole different chapter—the secret code and language that our kids use online. All right, just one more to give you a little clarity as to what's going on: *POS* means "Parent Over Shoulder," as in "Mom is reading everything I say, so keep it clean, asshole!" You might want to take a crash course!

"Change"

CHANGE HAPPENS, AND WE HAVE to learn, grow, and evolve.

"The only constant in life is change."
—François de La Rochefoucauld, French author

Try to approach every day as a challenge to improve. Don't be persistent in doing everything the way you always did. It's not a good formula for business or your personal life. The apes evolved, and look at us now! If you don't think change happens, then you missed 9/11. That day changed life as I knew it forever. It didn't ruin it, but it gave it more perspective. I view everything a little differently now. I think most of us do.

Because I am in the business of jobs, things got kind of difficult for a couple of years after, as companies reevaluated hiring and spending and started outsourcing jobs and restructuring. Watching those towers come down was the single saddest thing I ever witnessed, but in a strange way, it was also one of the more hopeful and optimistic days. Seeing Mayor Rudy Giuliani rally our great country against this axis of evil and not give in, to forget about the hatred, bigotry, racism, and come together as one. American flags hung from every house as far as the eye could see. (I still have my flag up and have had it up since September 12, 2001.) I feel a sense of patriotism that I never felt before. America is a truly great place to live. I heard Bono once say; "America is more than a nation, it's an idea." The idea that anything is possible!

Change happens all around us in different forms. We change jobs—or, more specifically, bosses, departments, positions, and locations. It's life's way of giving you a fresh chance at an opportunity to reinvent yourself. We are constantly asked to adjust and prove ourselves. Successfully adapting to change has more to do with a positive attitude and should be approached as an opportunity for self-motivation.

> **"Life is 10 percent what happens to you and 90 percent how you react to it."**
> **—Charles Swindoll, writer**

Be true to your values but receptive to change. We can't control when and how things will change, but we can control how we deal with it. If you see an open door, do you walk through it or run from it? Embrace change; don't fear it!

> **"If nothing ever changed, there'd be no butterflies."**
> **—Unknown**

Be willing to evolve and reinvent yourself. Seek new chapters and adventures in your life. Have the strength to exhibit resolve in the face of adversity and be willing to accept and embrace change. We are never too old to learn or improve.

> **"To improve is to change; to be perfect is to change often."**
> **—Winston Churchill**

Good can and does come from bad situations or imperfect origins—my everything-happens-for-a-reason philosophy. If "A" didn't happen, then we would never have had "B". You get the equation.

> **"When something bad happens, you have three choices. You can let it define you, let it destroy you, or you can let it strengthen you."**
> **—Unknown**

Life can change swiftly, and you must be willing to evolve. It's important to have a strong foundation and support system when change occurs.

> **"Castles made of sand melt into the sea eventually."**
> **—Jimi Hendrix, "The Ultimate Experience"**

We all need support, and it's hard to have to go it alone. There is no shame in the need for help or the willingness to accept it. Being receptive to assistance is healthy; dependency is not. A strong foundation is built over time. Trust is earned; respect is nurtured.

> **"May your hands always be busy, may your feet always be swift. May you have a strong foundation, when the winds of change shift."**
> **—Bob Dylan, "Forever Young"**

"Positive Outlook and Perspective"

THIS IS PERHAPS THE MOST important thing I have learned. Outlook and attitude is everything. I am an eternal optimist who chooses to be hopeful and view the world through rose-colored glasses. View the glass as half full instead of half empty. Optimistic people are generally happier than pessimists. A Mayo Clinic study found optimistic people live longer than pessimists. They tend to have conveniently shorter-term memories. Positive people take setbacks in stride, as temporary. Negative people view setbacks as permanent and harp on the potential ramifications, usually compounding the damage.

"Stay away from negative people. They have a problem for every solution."
—unknown

It's easier to adjust the equation than you think. Try to see the good in people by giving them the benefit of the doubt. Simply smiling at a stranger can make a difference. (You will be surprised how many people will smile back.) Kindness with a dash of charm can take you far in life. Don't believe conventional wisdom that nice guys finish last. It's been my observation that most successful people have achieved greater heights by being good at communicating with others.

The days of feeling that you have to be a mean boss to get results are long gone. Most people respond better to mutual respect and constructive criticism than to a harsh, negative approach. That's not to say that a supervisor should not set expectations high and hold people accountable for bottom line results. As long as a manager outlines his or her desired expectations up front, he or she can still create a positive, nurturing work environment without being taken advantage of.

Communication skills, or "soft skills," usually separate two candidates with the same skill set. Don't be afraid to be friendly and allow yourself to be interested in the thoughts of others. Once again, you will be surprised how much you can learn by listening. Body language can also convey a lot about a person. If you are on an interview, always be kind to the receptionist, as he or she is the first line of defense. Make sure your handshake is firm (not a vise grip) and try not to cross your arms. Avoid nodding excessively and try not to stare. Eye contact is essential to any conversation. If your eyes wander during the course of a conversation, it conveys lack of interest and focus, as well as a lack of confidence.

> **"Your smile is your logo, your personality is your business card, how you leave others feeling after an experience with you becomes your trademark."**
> **—Jay Danzie, author**

Make sure to do your homework and show your prospective employer that you are conscientious. The most important question a company will ask in an interview is what you know about their company. Don't be lazy; just don't! Be positive and act like you've been there before. Fake it until you make it! If you look and act successful, you will be viewed as such and, subsequently, make a better impression for upcoming opportunities. To attain success, you must project success. Think inside the box—that's right, I said "inside." You don't have to come up with the "big idea" or "reinvent the wheel" every day. Be the best that you can be at your current given position.

> **"Do what you gotta do so you can do what you wanna do."**
> **—Denzel Washington**

It will eventually give you the opportunity to move up and allow you to show your more creative side.

> **"Don't waste time learning the 'tricks of the trade.' Instead, learn the trade."**
> **—H. Jackson Brown Jr., author**

It takes about ten good years to become an "overnight success." Keep a positive outlook and be willing to work your way up from the bottom. Everyone has the ability to be positive, and the harder life is, the more important it is to keep the faith. I am not a very religious or spiritual person, although I wish I were. I think belief brings hope, and faith is hopeful. I do, however, believe in destiny and fate and firmly believe that things happen for a reason. It's always worked that way for me.

There's a great quote from the movie *Serendipity* when Dean (Jeremy Piven) writes a eulogy for his best friend, Jonathan (John Cusack), who "concluded that if we are to live life in harmony with the universe, we must all possess a powerful faith in what the ancients used to call 'fatum,' what we currently refer to as destiny." Dean goes on to say:

> **"Life is not merely a series of meaningless accidents or coincidences. Uh-uh. But rather it's a tapestry of events that culminate in an exquisite, sublime plan."**

A related quote comes from Marilyn Monroe:

> **"I believe that everything happens for a reason. People change so that you can learn to let go, things go wrong so that you appreciate them when they're right, you believe lies so you eventually learn to trust no one but yourself, and sometimes good things fall apart so better things can fall together."**

Every closed door can be an opportunity for a greater path. You simply have to believe and keep the faith—hey, maybe I do believe after all. I also firmly believe that destiny and fate play a big role in how our lives are defined. I don't believe that there is only one road or one true love. Like in the movie *Sliding Doors,* a brief second could change the rest of your life—a chance meeting, missing a train as the doors close—and define your eventual destiny. It could mean either meeting the person of your dreams or not. Here's a great line from the movie *Benjamin Button*:

> **"Our lives are defined by opportunities, even the ones we miss."**

It's confusing at best to know our true destiny. As Forrest Gump said in the movie of the same name:

> **"I don't know if we have a destiny or if we're all just floatin' around accidental-like on a breeze. But I, I think maybe it's both happening at the same time."**

Perspective is critical and usually comes with age. Things usually aren't as bad as they appear, and the future is up to you. Ever notice how things always appear so great in the past (the good old days)? We all have conveniently selective memories to help us feel good about ourselves.

> **"The good ole days weren't always good, and tomorrow ain't as bad as it seems."**
> **—Billy Joel, "Keeping the Faith"**

It's easy to complain or feel that you have been dealt a bad hand until you see a person with a true disability who shows perseverance. Within the word *disability* lies the word *ability*. Perception and outlook can define the way you view the two words. Jim Abbott, a one-handed pitcher for the New York Yankees who tossed a no-hitter in 1993, said the following while speaking about his disability:

> **"It's not the disability that defines you. It's how you deal with the challenges the disability presents you with. We have an obligation to the abilities we do have, not the disability. People will tell you that I overcame obstacles. Maybe.**

But the truth is, I was incredibly blessed in my life. More was given than was ever taken away."

That positive outlook and perseverance is truly inspiring, but it's not always easy to be so optimistic in the face of adversity. When it's your world, the littlest things feel (and are) important, but once again, it's all about perspective.

Inspirations

INSPIRATIONS, HEROES, AND ROLE MODELS lay the foundation and influence who we become as adults. For me, it's my grandparents. Because I didn't have a good relationship with my dad, my gramps was like my father and inspiration. When I was twenty-two, he passed away of a sudden heart attack at the age of sixty-eight, and I still honor him today. He worked hard and knew how to enjoy life. He took me to the horses, taught me how to play craps on a miniature Vegas craps table when I was eight (I still have the dice from the now-defunct Sands Hotel and keep them in my pocket for all important events for good luck), and raced me on the beach. He taught me the importance of working hard, enjoying life, and respecting others in the process. He was humble yet charismatic and confident with a unique zest for life.

"Heroes are people who rise to the occasion and slip away quietly."
—Tom Brokaw

Nan (as we called her) was even more inspiring with regard to how she handled his death. She picked herself up and decided to live the rest of her life just as he would have wanted and resumed her role as matriarch of our family. We all have choices. It's sad to see anyone with a zest for life just give up!

You can still have a special place in your heart for a loved one without feeling disloyal or guilty for moving on. I was fortunate and honored to be there holding her hand when she drew her last breath, and she honored me with a final smile as if to say, "Everything will be all right. Now you make the right choices!"

Too many people feel bad for themselves and wallow in self-pity. They feel like a victim if they had regrets as a kid. I chose to learn from my experiences and be a better father to my kids. I hate hearing about people who were abused as a kid and then, in turn, abuse their kid because they didn't feel they got a break. News flash: you are your father. Nothing could be more motivating or inspiring to me than not becoming my father.

Life is a team sport, and we all need mentors and inspirations in our lives. Even the occasional pat on the back can help more than you realize. People can also inspire without being completely inspirational. Sound confusing? You may find certain attributes of an individual's personality/characteristics inspiring without finding the complete individual inspirational. The separate parts don't always equal the whole. A great leader does not necessarily make a great person and vice versa. Listening and observing certain traits and skills of those around you can help you formulate the person you want to become. Be open-minded and receptive to different approaches. Choose those individual characteristics that you find to be successful and inspiring.

I don't have a problem with kids looking up to celebrities or athletes as heroes. After all, most of them did accomplish their success through hard work and sacrifice, even if they aren't what some would consider great role models. It would be refreshing, however, if more kids looked up to their parents or other family members as role models and heroes. More often than not, it's the hard work, sacrifice, and love of these individuals that enable the child to thrive and succeed. Again, not every parent is worthy of your inspiration, but try to search from within first. Inspirations are important, and we all need role models and heroes in our lives. The only problem is choosing the right ones can be a bit confusing today. Still Nan and Gramps for me!

"Character"

FEW THINGS ARE AS IMPORTANT as a person's character. Character encompasses all of our personality traits rolled into one and distinguishes us from one another. Here's a great line from the movie *Invincible*:

"Character is tested when you're up against it."

You can tell a lot about people from the way they handle adverse situations.

"Tough times don't last; tough people do."
—Robert Schiller, author

We are put to the test on a daily basis to make decisions that formulate the way people perceive us. The first rule I have as it relates to character is that you must believe in yourself. If you don't believe in yourself, how can you expect anyone else to believe in you? Set high expectations for yourself and care less about anyone else's expectations of you.

"Character is defined by what you do when no one is looking. What you do in the dark comes out in the light."
—Herm Edwards, NFL coach

If you try to spend your life trying to please others all the time, you will lose yourself in the process. Billy Jean King quoted William Shakespeare upon being immortalized in the recently renamed Billie Jean King National Tennis Center (US Open) by saying,

"To thine own self be true."

Believe in yourself and have the courage to stand by your convictions.

"If you don't stand for something, you will fall for anything."
—Malcolm X

King joined Arthur Ashe in being immortalized by our country's tennis headquarters. Neither was honored for being the best American tennis player; it was for the way they fought for human rights, battled for humanity, and displayed courage and character in the face of great adversity. We all find ourselves in difficult situations forced to make difficult decisions. We are put to the test on a daily basis to make decisions that we all take for granted. How should I dress? What's for lunch? Should I make a move on my colleague? You get the idea. Might as well make an informed decision instead of lying to yourself and not getting the preferred result. Not making a decision is in fact making a decision. I know—complicated at best. It's always easier to defer to the masses and make the popular choice. How do you handle it? Are you resilient? Do you persevere? Do you defer to the majority? Remember that giving in or giving up is always easier than having the power to stand by your convictions, especially if they are unpopular. Always let your conscience be your guide.

> **"Character cannot be developed in ease and quiet. Only through experience of trial and suffering can the soul be strengthened, vision cleared, ambition inspired, and success achieved."**
> **—Helen Keller**

Have the power to overcome negative perception. Care less about what people think and more about what you think. Be willing to fail, and you will have the ability to succeed.

> **"If you need somebody you can trust, trust yourself."**
> **—Bob Dylan, "Trust Yourself"**

Recently I found the following anonymous poem on the web:

> **If you think you are beaten, you are;**
> **If you think you dare not, you don't;**
> **If you'd like to win but you think you can't,**
> **You can almost be certain you won't.**
> **If you think that you'll lose, you are lost,**
> **For out in the world you will find**
> **Success begins with a person's will;**
> **It's all in the state of mind.**
> **If you think you're outclassed, you are;**
> **You've got to think high to rise.**
> **You've got to be sure of yourself**
> **Before you can win the prize.**
> **Life's battles don't always go**

To a stronger or faster man;
But sooner or later the person who wins
Is the person that THINKS they can.

The motivation and desire to win is what's important; winning is just a bonus. Success is a state of mind.

"Change your thoughts and you change your mind."
—Norman Vincent Peale, author

Set your expectations high but realistic. If your goals are too grand, you might not be able to see the finish line in clear sight. Confidence builds high self-esteem and can be liberating. Allow yourself to be accountable for your decisions. Learn to trust yourself and your own intuition. More often than not, our initial gut instincts are correct. We are all so concerned with perception and reputation that we disregard our gut instincts when we run the risk of making a mistake.

"Be more concerned with your character than
with your reputation. Your character is what you
really are while your reputation is merely what
others think you are."
—John Wooden, UCLA basketball coach

The key is to be willing to make mistakes and, more importantly, learn from them. The definition of insanity is:

"... doing the same thing over and over again
and expecting different results."
—Albert Einstein

Making the proper adjustments by trial and error allows you to grow with confidence. Experience and knowledge breed confidence! Try it; if you make a mistake, you can always blame it on the dog (Roxy) like I do! We all make mistakes, and the world around us has a shorter memory than you think. Others will soon forget about your mistake as soon as the next person makes his/hers (yesterday's news). What they might remember is that you had the guts and character to put yourself out there. Justin Trudeau, prime minister of Canada and son of Pierre Trudeau (beloved Canadian prime minister), who was also an amateur boxer, said:

"People think that boxing is all about how hard you can hit your opponent. It's not. Boxing is about how hard a hit you can take and keep going."

It's easy to say that we shouldn't care what anyone else thinks, but that's unrealistic in today's culture. We all want to be liked and strive for acceptance from our peers. Rejection affects confidence, and perception is reality. Be trustworthy, have respect for other opinions/decisions, and take responsibility for your own. Be willing to take a chance and be willing to fail—it's character building!

"A man's character is his fate."
—Heraclitus, Greek philosopher

Right to the point: we are all inevitably bound by the content of our character!

"Passion"

I HAVE ALWAYS BELIEVED THAT a life void of passion is an empty life. Passion makes you alive and full of energy. It's an overwhelming enthusiasm for any action. Sometimes you have to search for it, but rest assured, it is worth the search. Once again, "if you follow your passion, you will inevitably find your purpose." One of my favorite quotes is another line from the movie *Serendipity* in a scene where Dean (played by Jeremy Piven) gives a eulogy for his friend (played by John Cusack). He says:

> **"The Greeks never wrote obituaries. When a man died, they asked only one question, 'Did he have a passion?'"**

Once again, straight and to the point, yes or no, did he or didn't he? I like that thinking, and I recommend the movie. No one pulls off a sappy movie like John Cusack. (I also love *Say Anything* and *The Sure Thing*.) The other quote is less current. It is by the German Poet Christian Friedrich Hebbel. He said:

> **"Nothing great in the world has ever been accomplished without passion."**

It can't get simpler than that! Whatever you do in life, do it with passion and give it 100 percent. Don't settle for less, and don't let people tell you what you can and can't achieve.

> **"If you get out of your own way ... it is amazing what will come to you."**
> **—Laird Hamilton, professional surfer**

No one said it would be easy—nothing worth a damn ever is.

> **"The road to easy street goes through the sewer."**
> **—John Madden**

Pay attention to the three Ps: passion, patience, and persistence. Indulge your passions, understand that nothing happens right away, and "keep pushin' till it's understood," to once again quote Bruce Springsteen. Passionate people are more alive, more determined, and more willing to take risks. They believe in themselves and are willing to fail for the chance to succeed. Some are passionate about one thing, but I find most passionate people find passion a way of life. They exude more positive energy and find more excitement about life in general. If something is worth doing, then it's worth doing it the best way possible. So much talent is unrequited due to a lack of confidence and belief in themselves. The passion, not necessarily the skill, defines success.

> **"Nothing is more common than unsuccessful people with talent."**
> **—Calvin Coolidge, US president**

Don't give in to your fear or your lack of determination. In the movie *The Shawshank Redemption*, a character observes:

"Fear can keep you prisoner; hope can set you free."

Tomorrow is a new day. Wake up and get going! If you reach for the skies, you might not achieve your goal, but you might find you achieve more then you thought possible.

> **"You can't always get what you want, but if you try sometime you just might find, you get what you need."**
> **—Rolling Stones, "You Can't Always Get What You Want"**

I need to group spirit in this section with passion, as I believe they are linked. Inner and outer spirit usually go hand in hand with passionate people. I was speaking to this woman with tattoos and piercings all over her body and had an epiphany during our conversation. There are people who wear their tattoos on the outside and those who wear theirs on the inside. I never judge people and like to observe and find out what's behind the tattoos. I concluded that I wear many tattoos on the inside and sometimes wish they were visible. How about you?

Service

SERVICE IS THE SINGLE MOST important aspect of any business. That being said, why are so many business owners so shortsighted? They invest everything they have in a business and forget the most important fact—that the customer is paying the bills. I wish more people took pride in what they did and were a bit more courteous.

If I frequent a restaurant often, I want the owner or maître d' to acknowledge me. I'm not saying you have to give me anything, but at least acknowledge me and make me feel special—even if I'm not. That said, no matter how special I feel, if the food and service aren't consistent, it doesn't matter.

I'm a sucker for good service and tip accordingly. Tipping is discretionary, so I allow the quality of the service to dictate the discretion. Look, I didn't ask you to be a waiter, and I don't care if you're between careers. Just treat me with good service, and I don't mean when you bring the check.

> **"To give real service, you must add something which cannot be bought or measured with money, and that is sincerity and integrity."**
> **—Douglas Adams, author**

Don't you hate that? I would rather someone be discourteous all the way through rather than smile at the end. I don't like being played for a fool. I like to over tip, because it means I had a good experience.

I once had the absolute worst service (you know the kind) and left the waitress a 5 percent tip. I wanted to get my point across and saw no reason to encourage bad service by tipping the appropriate amount. The secret is out—you sucked! When I was leaving the restaurant, the waitress approached me with her manager, and the manager asked me if everything was okay. I wasn't really in the mood for a scene, so I said "yes" and started to walk away. I thought to myself, *No, it really wasn't okay*, so I turned around and said, "Now that you ask, *no!*" (How dare this waitress question me after that effort?) I then told the manager and anyone in earshot that it was the absolute worst service I had ever had, and she had ruined an otherwise nice evening. I was offended that she had the nerve to approach me when she knew that she was lucky to have received a penny. The waitress went white; her manager apologized and let me know that she would try harder next time. I thanked her and got in my car. I've never been back.

Take pride in what you do, whatever you do. Be the best waitress, teacher, or CEO that you can be. People aren't stupid, and you will be rewarded in the end. Maybe not right away, but just maybe that CEO you waited on and who took a liking to you speaks to a friend of his who is looking for a relationship manager and thinks you would be great. That's how life works. Take pride and don't be shortsighted. Just don't! Don't settle for mediocrity when you can give something 100 percent.

"Mediocrity's easy / the good things take time / the great need commitment."
—Bob Seger, "Lock and Loaded"

"Balance"

WITH A TYPICAL AMERICAN WORKING fifty-plus hours a week, how is it possible to balance work, family, and diet? Answer: choices! Overworking and earning more doesn't equate to success—not at the cost of time spent with your kids or your spouse.

> **"Ninety percent of being a dad is just showing up."**
> **—Jay Pritchett, *Modern Family***

Times are different than our parents' generation. They say (I still don't know who *they* are, but I like them a lot more now) that the fifties are the new forties and the forties are the new thirties. I couldn't agree more! Life is truly different than our parents' generation. We have more information at our fingertips but seem to have very selective methods of using it. It seems that we are a more health-conscious society but still lack the self-discipline to benefit from all that knowledge. Once again, it comes down to deciding what is most important. Balance is extremely difficult, because it takes trade-offs. We want it all and are not interested in making concessions or sacrifices. Prioritizing can be a difficult task. You first need to identify what choices will make you happiest.

> **"It's a helluva start, being able to recognize what makes you happy."**
> **—Lucille Ball**

For me, it comes down to family first. My wife and I have made decisions together that have come with certain sacrifices. It is especially difficult for women. It seems like a lose-lose situation! If a woman works and does not spend as much time with her children as possible, she will have guilt. If a woman doesn't work and the family needs the income to better their life and that of their children, then there is the guilt of not doing everything possible for the children's future. Sarah Jessica Parker starred in a funny movie about a working mom, *I Don't Know How She Does It*, in which she compared a working woman's head to the control tower at O'Hare Airport. Her character spoke of having two lives and being no good at either one of them. What is the best decision? That, my friends, is the million-dollar question. There is no right or wrong answer. You simply have to make decisions with your spouse (or partner) that you feel comfortable with, and you can't beat yourself up. Guess what? You will likely make mistakes. And guess what else? You can decide to change your mind. Nothing is forever, and what seems important to you today may be vastly different down the road. Make the most educated choices that you can and reserve the right to change your mind.

> **"I've learned that you can't have everything and do everything at the same time."**
> **—Oprah Winfrey**

Balance is the single most difficult thing for any person or family to achieve. Inevitably, you will have to give something up. Coming to terms with that can be very tricky. Just decide!

"Dimension"

BEING WELL-ROUNDED AND THREE-DIMENSIONAL IS important to a healthy lifestyle. If someone is fulfilled in his or her personal and work life, chances are he or she will also maintain a healthy lifestyle. Get off the couch and find an outlet. Take up art, photography, the theatre, or sports. It's easy to fall into the trap of being lazy and nonproductive. An active lifestyle breeds a healthier, more mentally challenging, and more productive life. Outlets tend to relieve some of your day-to-day stress. They allow you to focus on something other than the daily grind that we all incur. I'm not saying that a little relaxation like watching TV is all bad. We all need some mindless activity to unwind with. Just make sure it does not prevail.

I am an advocate of couples having independent interests. I still play basketball, softball, and golf with my friends and then go to the bar for a couple of cold ones after to rehash the game. At my age, rehashing takes on a life of its own. (You guys know what I mean.) Occasional boys-only golf trips or girls-only spa trips are recommended. We all need to recharge our batteries, and like "they" say, absence makes the heart grow fonder. There has to be a mutual trust between partners for any relationship to have a chance.

> **"Don't smother each other. No one can grow in the shade."**
> **—Leo Buscaglia, author**

The more well-rounded and three-dimensional you each are, the more relaxed and patient you will be with each other. Patience is a virtue that comes with age. Apparently, I am not yet old enough! We are an impatient culture that wants it all, and we want it now. I hear that yoga or meditation help, only I don't have the patience to try. Anything worth a damn in life takes time. The millennial generation has a sense of entitlement and an expectation of life going as planned—instantaneous delivery of the life they have chosen. They don't realize that anything great takes both patience and time.

"Patience is power."
—Stephanie Hirsch, artist

One dimension of my personality that has developed with age is my sensitive and emotional side. I have become much sappier. It used to take a good *Brian's Song* to get me to weep; now I well up at cheesy commercials. (What's that all about?) I think, as we get older, we become more sensitive to life, family, and our own mortality. Come on, please don't tell me it's only me. Misery loves company, and it would help to know that many of you feel just as sappy. Since you didn't answer, I will take that as a yes!

"Risk"

TAKING CALCULATED RISKS ALLOWS YOU to aspire to reach higher goals. Not everyone is built for risk. Some like the safe, consistent path through life. Some are eternal optimists. Powerball players, who love a thrill, fear missing out. Risk makes your heart flutter and your blood rush. Gambling and taking a calculated risk are very different. Gambling requires a bit more luck and hope than calculated risk-taking. Diversifying your portfolio with 10 to 15 percent in riskier investments makes sense to me—at the appropriate age—and gives you a little something to hope for (do your research or hire someone who does). If you balance the rest of it in safe or fixed investments, the down side is negligible.

> **"Take calculated risks. That is quite different from being rash."**
> **—George Patton**

In general, most people are willing to settle for safe instead of taking a chance. Don't be afraid to fail, or you already have.

> **"In the end, what we regret most are the chances we never took."**
> **—Frasier Crane, *Frasier***

Try out for that sport in high school. Don't let someone tell you that you aren't good enough. Have self-confidence and be willing to fail. If there was a sure way to confirm your gut instincts, then it wouldn't be a risk.

> **"No great discovery was ever made without a bold guess."**
> **—Isaac Newton**

Stand up and do the public speaking that you have feared for years. Fear can consume and overwhelm, and the longer you give in, the harder it gets to take the chance.

> **"Life begins at the end of your comfort zone."**
> **—Neale Donald Walsch, author**

You need to be fearless and scared at the same time. Just make sure your passion for the moment overrides your fear.

> **"Everything you've ever wanted is on the other side of fear."**
> **—George Addair, humanitarian**

Keep your inner desire for security aside, because if you play things too safe, you will inevitably lose the security that you seek.

> **"Ever notice that 'what the hell' is always the right decision?"**
> **—Marilyn Monroe**

Remain positive and confident in the face of fear. If you waiver or give in, then you will not be able to commit to your desired outcome.

"When your confidence fades, can you carry yourself on through? When you wake from a dream, can you make that dream come true?"
—Michael Pollack, "Chances Are"

Every now and again you need to allow your spirit of adventure to win the day over common sense.

"Sometimes common sense ain't that common."
—Steve Harvey, comedian and talk-show host

Forget about the past and focus on the present. I relate it to golf (everything relates to golf): forget about the bad shot you just hit (you can't do anything about it unless you cheat) and focus on the ball sitting right in front of you and your next shot (don't compound your mistakes). We are all presented with a handful of defining moments in the course of our lives that inevitably shape our future—the proverbial fork in the road.

"When you come to a fork in the road, take it."
—Yogi Berra

It's always easier to take a risk when you're young than to regret not having had the guts when you're older.

"We are all faced with a series of great opportunities brilliantly disguised as impossible situations."
—Charles Swindoll, writer

You don't need years of therapy to overcome your past. Be willing to have the confidence to change your approach and take a calculated risk. We all have choices and the option to change our minds.

> **"Yes, there are two paths you can go by, but in the long run there's still time to change the road you're on."**
> **—Led Zeppelin, "Stairway to Heaven"**

What's done is done, and life is too short to concentrate on things that you cannot change. It's what you do next that counts. If resolution for you means approaching someone in the past to come to terms and put closure to an event, then do it and move on.

> **"We are products of our pasts, but we don't have to be prisoners of it."**
> **—Rick Warren, author**

Don't spend the rest of your life feeling sorry for yourself, or you have allowed that person to continue whatever abuse was inflicted. It really is as easy as that. I think people use therapy as a crutch.

> **"Don't use the past as an excuse to miss out on your future."**
> **—Alan Cohn, author**

Again, I am not saying that some form of therapy can't be helpful in the right situation; just display good judgment. One type of therapy that makes sense to me is solution-focused brief therapy (SFBT). SFBT focuses on what the patient wants to achieve through therapy rather than on the problems that made them seek help in the first place. This approach focuses on the present and future rather than dwelling on the past. For you *Fifty Shades* lovers, SFBT is the therapy that Dr. Flynn used on Christian Grey in the second book of the trilogy, *Fifty Shades Darker*.

Hell, sometimes it's worth going to the ponies just to get the blood flowing. I personally like to gamble. I never bet a lot or over my head, just a little something to have the action. It makes things a bit more exciting and interesting to me. I'm not encouraging you to start a life of gambling, but do something in your life that makes you feel more alive and fulfilled.

"Do one thing every day that scares you."
—Eleanor Roosevelt

Just try it!

Leadership

"Great leaders are aware and attuned to themselves, to others, and to the world around them. They commit to their beliefs, stand strong in their values, and live full, passionate lives. Great leaders are emotionally intelligent. They inspire through demonstrating passion and commitment, and a deep concern for the people they lead."
—Richard Boyatzis, leadership author

If you are comfortable with yourself and are committed and passionate, people will follow.

"Be yourself, because everyone else is taken."
—Oscar Wilde, writer and poet

People want to assimilate, have commonality, and, most importantly, trust their leaders. They want to be secure that the ideals of the people they follow are similar in nature to their own. I am a sucker for someone I feel is real, with a unique and idealistic approach. So many leaders today deliver a political "party line" that seems so rehearsed. They say what they think we want to hear. Again, don't take me for a fool! Is it just me, or has all political campaigning become one big negative smear campaign? I don't want to hear candidates spend all of their time and money trashing their opponents' credibility. I want them to speak to their own accomplishments and furnish me with the information necessary to warrant my support.

> **"Some would say I was a lost man in a lost world.**
> **You could say I lost my faith in the people on TV.**
> **You could say I'd lost my belief in our politicians.**
> **They all seemed like game-show hosts to me."**
> **—Sting, musician**

I don't have a list of criteria by which I pick my leaders; however, I do have one for my president. He should be smarter than me. I'm not mentioning any names, but I'm not sure that some of our recent candidates fit the criteria. A leader by definition is someone we choose to follow.

> **"Good leadership isn't about advancing yourself.**
> **It's about advancing your team."**
> **—John C. Maxwell, author**

I think people respond to leaders with heart and passion and a vision and plan to implement it. They listen to the people they represent.

> **"Leaders who don't listen will eventually be surrounded by people who have nothing to say."**
> **—Andy Stanley, pastor**

This applies to our direct supervisors as well as our politicians. I don't believe that all of our leaders should be clones of each other. It's important to have your own personality and style.

I have found it helpful to mirror certain aspects of people I have observed along the way. I don't believe it's a good idea to try to copy any one person's style 100 percent. Integrate aspects of different character traits that you have observed to be successful and combine them with your own unique style. Remember, listening and learning from those who inspire you can help you formulate the person you want to become. I'd like to think I was a good mixture of traits from Jax Teller (*Sons of Anarchy*), Hank Moody (*Californication*), and Jerry Seinfeld. Fun-loving, well-intended, sometimes reckless, always sarcastic, with a family-first approach to life. Be true to yourself and develop your own individual style.

> **"Be who you are and say what you feel because those who mind don't matter and those who matter don't mind."**
> **—Dr. Seuss**

Don't be someone else's idea of what you should be. Just don't.

> **"Well I try my best to be just like I am, but everybody wants you to be just like them."**
> **—Bob Dylan, "Maggie's Farm"**

Humor

WE ARE ALL TOO AWARE of how serious and stressful life can be. That said, few things are healthier than a good belly laugh.

"I am thankful for laughter, except when milk comes out of my nose."
—Woody Allen

A good sense of humor can be healthy and, from what the ladies say, attractive as well. (See, you macho guys have been going about things the wrong way!) Self-deprecating humor shows that you are comfortable with your flaws and not self-conscious. It has always been in vogue to laugh, and few things are as universal as laughter. Who doesn't like going to a good comedy club or watching a funny movie? Laughter is truly contagious (one of the few things worth catching).

That same comical attitude can be applied to life in most situations. We all need to be a little less uptight and be willing to laugh at ourselves. Most comedy is funnier to me when I can relate it to my day-to-day mishaps. You will notice that your hardier laughter comes at the expense of yourself. *Seinfeld* is a classic example of this kind of humor and my favorite TV sitcom of all time. I can pretty much recite every line before it comes (not sure that really speaks volumes for me).

A timely sense of humor can diffuse a tense situation at work, lending a certain confidence. I do have one question. I happen to have a good memory, so why is it so hard to remember a joke? Ever notice that? Some people can rattle off ten at a time; I can't remember one. Of course, some people can remember the joke but have no clue how to tell it. A joke can also have underlying meaning that can educate the ignorant. I recently received the following joke in an e-mail from a friend;

> **Two bored casino croupiers were waiting at the craps table. A very attractive blonde woman from Alabama arrived and bet twenty thousand dollars on a single roll of the dice. She said, "I hope you don't mind, but I feel much luckier when I play topless." With that, she stripped to the waist, rolled the dice, and yelled, "Come on, baby! Southern girl needs new clothes!" As the dice came to a stop, she jumped up and down and squealed, "Yes! Yes! I won! I won!" She hugged the croupiers and then picked up her winnings and her clothes and quickly departed. The croupiers stared at each other dumbfounded. Finally, one of them asked, "What did she roll?" The other answered, "I don't know. I thought you were watching."**

Moral: Not all Southerners are stupid. Not all blondes are dumb. But all men are men. It's a funny joke, but the real meaning to me is that we shouldn't be so quick to judge people or think we know it all. People can surprise you with their depth and dimension if you allow them the opportunity. Be open-minded. Don't believe stereotypes or be quick to judge a book by its cover.

> **"Don't judge a picture by the frame; every man is not the same."**
> **—Elton John, "Understanding Women"**

Life is serious enough without the extra drama. Try taking the little things a little less seriously and find a way to laugh at yourself.

> **"Life is too important to take seriously."**
> **—Oscar Wilde, author**

A simple smile can change the perception of the people around you. Like I said: smile, and the world might just smile back. Try it!

"Relationships"

Now THIS IS A DIFFICULT topic, but I am going to give you advice right now that will be sure to change your life for the better. We all suffer from relationships that go bad or just disappear over time. We really aren't sure why and can't remember the root cause half the time. Life just gets busy, and it's easier not to remember than to make an effort to mend. Everyone reading this book knows exactly what I mean. It's a lot easier to forget than to remember.

Many times it's just a matter of time, and life getting the best of us. The longer you don't speak, the harder it gets to reconnect and the easier it gets to forget. Now for the tricky part and the truth—we never really forget, and it haunts us all. None of us likes unresolved relationships, especially when we are as much at fault. It's easier not to deal than to make the call.

> **"When something is missing in your life, it usually turns out to be someone."**
> **—Robert Brault, writer**

Think of how great you would feel getting "the call"—from the relative you always loved but had a brief falling out with or the friend you had that little disagreement with. It's silly stuff most of the time, but we would all rather shy away from confrontation, even at the risk of losing the relationship. Facing the fallout bears the reminder of our own imperfections.

Well, some relationships are better left for dead, and we all know which ones they are. Those are not the ones we struggle over. It's the relationships that we get reminded of from time to time that leave us with empty guilt. Here's the solution: pick up the phone and let the other person know that it doesn't matter what happened all those years ago and you want him or her back in your life. The person will likely cry and tell you how great he or she feels that you reached out. Forgiveness and compassion for others can help relieve depression, stress, and anxiety within.

I personally have come to terms with forgiving my father, as I found out later in life that he suffers from bipolar disorder, which was not a diagnosed illness all those years ago. In essence, forgiving him is forgiving myself for not being able to save him. The conflict is sometimes within ourselves and not with another. Don't give depression a permanent address! There is true freedom in forgiveness.

As we get older, we realize that there is just not enough time. It's not the quantity; it's the quality. I can see a friend once every three years, and we always pick up exactly where we left off. Those are the relationships worth fighting for. Then you have that friend who no matter how often you call, it's never enough. Those are usually the needy friends who have not moved on.

> **"Sometimes you have to move on without certain people. If they're meant to be in your life, they will catch up."**
> **—Mandy Hale, author**

Nurture the real relationships and fight for them. Don't be stubborn and unrelenting. Guess what? You are only punishing yourself in the end. It's just not the same going to a funeral to make closure.

> **"If you were going to die soon and had only one phone call you could make, who would you call and what would you say? And why are you waiting?"**
> **—Stephen Levine, poet**

Do it when it counts—life is too short. Sound familiar? Are you tearing up as you think of that friend or sibling or parent or whomever? This is a wake-up call for you. Be the bigger person and make the first move. You won't regret it—just do it!

Romantic relationships and dating are completely different topics. Dating takes confidence, and rejection breeds inadequacy. We all want to feel desired and attractive, and we thirst for acceptance. A few bad dating experiences can quickly set a person back to the comforts of their couch with a pint of Häagen-Dazs firmly in hand. I've never been disappointed by a pint of Coffee Häagen-Dazs—can't say the same for dating! I recently watched a pretty bad chick flick, *He's Just Not That Into You*, in which a character played by Drew Barrymore speaks of getting rejected in today's technology-based world.

> **"I had this guy leave me a voice mail at work so I called him at home and then he e-mailed me to my BlackBerry and so I texted to his cell. And now you just have to go around checking all these different portals just to get rejected by seven different technologies. It's exhausting."**

If you take control of your life and your physical health, you will find a renewed level of confidence with your partner(s). If you don't take care of yourself and you feel unattractive, you can't expect anyone else to feel different. It affects the way you speak and act. It affects your body language and your self-confidence. If you are happy in your career and feel good about your self-image, your body language reflects the confidence. You will be more relaxed, more willing to have a sense of humor, and more decisive. It won't give you a square jaw, enable you to grow four inches, or give you a full head of hair, but it might make you feel as if it does.

Another problem with regard to dating is that we all have conveniently selective hearing. We all hear what we want to hear. Look for the signals and take your cues. Don't make your date spell it out for you; it's far more embarrassing in the end. When she says, "You are a pig, and I never want to see you again," that might be the first clue that it's probably not meant to be.

> **"When someone shows you who they are, believe them the first time."**
> **—Maya Angelou, poet**

Have a positive self-image and believe in yourself. Don't allow yourself to believe that you are not worthy of more.

> **"We accept the love we think we deserve."**
> **—Charlie, *The Perks of Being a Wallflower***

I don't have specific experience with regard to online dating, as I have been with my wife for more than thirty-five years, but my logical thoughts are that it's important to check out the reliability of the sites you use, don't meet strangers in strange places, and keep your information confidential. False advertising doesn't help anyone, so don't doctor your pictures. The initial disappointment of a meeting could damage your confidence for future dating. That doesn't mean putting in a bad picture. Give yourself the best chance possible, but if you can't re-create the picture, you could be in for a long night or a very short one. It shouldn't be all about appearance, but you may not get the chance to show your partner all of your other great qualities if there's not an initial attraction. First impressions are important.

"You never get a second chance at a first impression."
—Eleanor Roosevelt

I quote that to all of the people I send out on interviews. Take nothing for granted, and always put your best foot forward. It will likely distinguish you from the field. The rest is up to you!

Long-term relationships and marriage take compromise and a willingness to adjust your selfish way of thinking. It sounds rough, but the truth hurts. No good relationship is always going to be good. You must be attracted to your partner or spouse, but you will need a great deal more once the initial honeymoon phase comes to an end and you are left with a person you have little in common with and no respect for. I am convinced that the secret of my successful relationship with my wife is that we both root for each other. We are each other's biggest fans. You marry someone at one stage in both your lives, and you sign on for the changes that lie ahead. You choose to grow together or you will surely grow apart. You need to like the one you love!

My favorite TV character, Hank Moody of *Californication*, was asked why he loves his girlfriend (and mother of his daughter) so much, and this was his response:

> **"I don't know. I don't think I have ever known. I think sometimes you get it right at the first time, and then it defines your life. It becomes who you are."**

We have been Stacy and Steven ever since!

Another favorite snippet from *Californication* comes when an older man shares some relationship wisdom with Hank:

> **"Well you know, it takes time. But once you get on the other side of all, having a friend to hold your hand while life kicks you in the ass and reminds you that that body of yours is just a loan."**

Don't even consider entering a long-term relationship or marriage unless you are willing to be exposed. You have to be vulnerable and put yourself out there to have a chance. In poker terms, you need to go "all in". That said, few things are more rewarding than living your life and parenting with a great partner.

> **"Lots of people want to ride with you in the limo, but what you want is someone who will take the bus with you when the limo breaks down."**
> **—Oprah Winfrey**

Marriage is a partnership. You must respect the person you are with and be willing to look at things from a different perspective and viewpoint. It's okay to disagree, and fighting is not optional—it is guaranteed. Just make sure you don't miss out on the makeup sex like George Costanza did on *Seinfeld*. Look, life is not easy, and it only makes sense that you will take out your daily frustrations on those you are closest to. It's easy to fall into a rut and far harder to climb out. Just don't make it a habit.

"Spend less time worrying who's right and more time deciding what's right."
—H Jackson Brown Jr., author

Attack the issues rather than the individual. Figure out what's more important, being happy or being right. You may win the battle, but that victory may come at a great expense. Learn how to take a deep breath before speaking. Most marital disagreements don't have a solution. Be prepared to compromise and simply agree to disagree.

Communication is the key to any lasting relationship. If you don't communicate a problem to your partner, how can you hold that person accountable? It makes sense to most men; however, it's my experience that women don't want to have to tell you what they are thinking. It is our job to know and to fix it!

"Man is a knot into which relationships are tied."
—Antoine de Saint-Exupéry, French poet

That said, once you have acknowledged and resolved the problem, the ensuing discussion of the resolved problem becomes more important than the consequential solution. Exactly! Good luck with that. So do special and spontaneous things. Keep the relationship fresh—try a new position. (No, I am not referring to a career position.) Planning for the future is difficult and stressful and limits your ability to be spontaneous, but just try! A little bit goes a long way!

As for sex and intimacy, I'm not going to get specific, as this book is probably embarrassing enough to my kids, and we all know about "the act." It's about acting with intelligence, not "the act" itself. Quite simply, women need foreplay, and I don't mean just in bed. It's about opening a car door or surprising her with flowers or a thoughtful gift, even—change that, *especially*—when it's not an occasion. People will tell you not to sweat the small stuff. Paying close attention to the details will not go unnoticed and your efforts will be rewarded when it counts. It will let your partner know that you are paying attention. And from what the ladies say, nothing is more attractive to a woman than a man who cares enough to listen. Change up the routine and bring passion and excitement back. Over time, a relationship gets stale just the way it is. Enter kids, and you can forget about spontaneity. That's when the unexpected is the most appreciated. The daily stress of life and raising a family is overwhelming to all, but a little bit of thought goes a long, long way.

Men are primitive beings with limited capacity. Forcing the issue can exacerbate the stress and be counterintuitive to the end goal. Let her see that you are sensitive to her needs and thoughtful to her wants. Don't get me wrong—I am still a work in progress, as my wife will be the first to tell you. I'd like to think that I have evolved over time and learned from my mistakes, but just when you start to feel comfortable, a woman will let you know where you failed. Just saying! Oh, and you probably did!

"Friendship"

I AM BLESSED AND FORTUNATE to have a lot of good friends. I live close to where I grew up, and many of my best friends have achieved a similar level of success and live in close proximity. We still play ball and socialize as families. The new friendships that I have made revolve around my children's friends' parents. It comes down to schedules and exposure.

Unlike family, we do have the luxury of picking our friends. My favorite friendship song is "No Surrender" by Bruce Springsteen, which is a love song to his best friend and first lead guitarist, Stevie Van Zandt. Here is a line from the chorus:

"We made a promise we swore we'd always remember, no retreat, baby, no surrender"

Unfortunately, the same can't be said about your partner or spouse's friends. The barometer for lasting friendships usually lies with your partner/spouse.

If they don't get along, forget it and maintain a separate boys/girls-only relationship.

Asking your spouse to develop a friendship with an alien will usually negatively impact your own relationship. Your spouse will resent being put in a continuously uncomfortable situation. Just because your friend is nice does not mean that the spouse follows suit. Spending the night with the arrogant and obnoxious spouse of one of my wife's friends is too much to ask, and I have decided that my free time is too precious to waste with people I neither like nor respect.

> **"Don't waste words on people who deserve your silence. Sometimes the most powerful thing you can say is nothing at all."**
> **—Mandy Hale, author**

The most valuable asset we have is our time, and how we choose to spend it is our choice!

> **"One of the most expensive things you could ever do is pay attention to the wrong people."**
> **—Anonymous**

I'm not saying that you shouldn't compromise at times, but please! Your friends are a reflection of yourself and usually share similar values. They are a barometer for other choices that we make in our lives.

A true friend is someone whom you can count on in a crisis and who loves you unconditionally (warts and all).

> **"A friend is someone who gives you total freedom to be yourself."**
> **—Jim Morrison**

Good friends tell you the truth, even when it hurts—change that, "especially when it hurts." We all need honest opinions that don't always reflect our own. Constructive criticism is great, but that being said, we don't need someone to continuously point out our flaws and constantly judge us. If your relationship becomes based on negative energy, it might be time to let your friend know how you feel.

"Let people know what you stand for—and what you won't stand for."
—H. Jackson Browne Jr., author

Open communication is always the key. If your friend becomes overly defensive and continuously critical, it might be time to move on. If you don't focus on your flaws, then why would you allow anyone else to? People change and do grow apart. Recognizing the difference between constructive and destructive friendships can be hard, but time brings clarity.

"People change and forget to tell each other."
—Lillian Hellman, author

Friendships create a foundation for your life. The people you choose to spend your precious free time with are a true reflection of who you are.

"A friend is someone who reaches for your hand ... but touches your heart."
—Anonymous

Life is busy, time is precious, and we have enough natural stress and drama without choosing relationships that add to it. I like to surround myself with people who make me laugh and share and understand my sarcastic and playful sense of humor.

"We don't stop playing because we grow old; we grow old because we stop playing."
—George Bernard Shaw, Irish playwright

Friends can be broken down into three categories: the ones you confide in, the ones you might confide in, and the ones you definitely won't confide in. They all play separate but important roles in our lives. Which one are you?

"Honesty"

THIS MAY SOUND WRONG, BUT it's been my experience that honesty is not always the best policy. Let me explain before you judge me. People don't really want to hear the *total* truth. I am not talking about the big stuff, but little white lies or fibs can be harmless and quite helpful to relationships. For example, say your wife asks you, "Honey, does my ass look fat in these jeans?" Not only do you lie, but you lie as fast as possible. If there's any form of hesitation, you might as well tell the truth, because not only are you in trouble, but you're also a liar. Sometimes the truth hurts, and we need to tactfully temper our verbal comments when we run the risk of being unnecessarily harsh.

The truth in many circumstances can have unintended negative consequences. Considering someone's feelings, before rendering your opinion can speak more about compassion than honesty. Giving others consideration and kindness rather than the harsh truth in many instances can also reveal strong character. The ancient Greek philosopher Plato was quoted as saying:

"Honesty is for the most part less profitable than dishonesty."

Now hold on. I don't believe Plato was suggesting that you should lie to your client/customer as it relates to business. I interpret this to mean—and I agree—that you should think before over-sharing and asking questions that you might not want the answer to. You don't owe your clients/customers all the gory details; you owe them a quality and timely result. We all get so caught up in the minutia. The minutia is your problem, not your clients' or customers' problem. (That's what they pay you for.) Less is more, and too much information, in many circumstances, can be very overrated! White lies and fibs aside, the truth is always the best policy. Integrity is becoming a rare trait today. With our politicians consistently talking out of both sides of their mouths, who can we really trust anyway?

> **"No man has a good enough memory to make a successful liar."**
> **—Abraham Lincoln**

Lies start small but grow fast, and the line becomes very blurred. One lie quickly becomes two, and before long, it is difficult to determine the truth.

> **"Always tell the truth. That way, you don't have to remember what you said."**
> **—Mark Twain, author**

"Diet and Exercise"

THEY (ANY GUESSES?) WANT YOU to believe that all these fad diets—calorie counting, fat calculating, etc.—can help you lose weight. Let me make this really simple. We are a society of excuses, justifications, and excesses. Just stop eating the crap that you convince yourself is okay. It's not, and you *know* it's not! If you simply cut back your portions and kept consistent, you will automatically and dramatically lose weight.

People today trick themselves into believing what they want to believe. We all know that supersize is not wise. When asked into how many pieces he wanted his pizza cut into, Yogi Berra replied:

"Four. I don't think I can eat eight."

Ya gotta love the guy! Simply changing the size of your plate can potentially alter your mindset. A smaller plate won't feel as empty, and conversely, you will feel more satisfied while eating less. If you need a shovel rather than a spoon, that could be the first sign of a problem! Yes, it's better to cut out the bread. Try water or flavored club soda instead of juices and sodas with sugar and additives, but if you like them, drink them—just use moderation.

Tapas—the Spanish concept of eating smaller portions of fine cuisine—is a great way to enjoy food without overeating.

The serving of tapas encourages conversation and allows the body to digest and register if you are full before you overeat. It's also a more social and healthier way to go.

Exercise is the key ingredient, and any exercise is good exercise. It helps to get some initial guidance, but you don't need to pay a personal trainer to scream at you for an hour to get the job done. Well, some of you might!

> **"The only exercise some people get is jumping to conclusions, running down their friends, sidestepping responsibility, and pushing their luck!"**
> **—Unknown**

Everything in life is better in moderation. Less is more. Stop looking to Dr. Phil to run your life. Show a little self-control and self-motivation; it can be quite liberating. You know the way—just stop being so dependent. We have become a culture of dependency.

I have worked hard with little assistance to build a business through a lot of frustration, many mistakes, and a bit of luck. Guess what? You can do everything right, and you still need a bit of good luck—not that you should rely on luck, because I am convinced you make your own luck. *Luck* can be defined as "Labor Under Constant Knowledge." Life is a numbers game; the harder and smarter you work, the better your chance of success. Don't look to those lottery winners to decide your career path or inevitable fate. Make your own luck and hope to get a bit along the way.

> **"I'm a great believer in luck, and I find the harder I work, the more I have of it."**
> **—Thomas Jefferson**

If you do take my advice (and I promise not to make you walk on a bed of hot coals to find your inner strength) and just *stop*, you will see that it will change your outlook. You will look better, feel and exude more confidence, and be better equipped and spirited to be a good mother, father, boss, or whatever it is that you want to improve at. If your pants are too tight, then you need to start. It's that simple. (And I'm not talking about your fat pants—you know what I mean.)

> **"It is never too late to be what you might have been."**
> **—George Eliot, Novelist**

Take a couple of weeks and just cut back. Don't lie to yourself; moderation will lead the way. Don't rationalize yourself into thinking that you're too busy to start right away. If you do delay, you will eventually wish you had started today.

> **"If you had started doing anything two weeks ago, by today you would have been two weeks better at it."**
> **—John Mayer, musician**

If you simply do push-ups and sit-ups, run or walk, and eat healthy, you don't need any weights or a gym to get the job done. Isometrics or resistance bands are great if you have limited space or travel a lot. Actually, spending about forty-five minutes to an hour exercising between your run and workout will do, but don't forget to stretch out first. Because most of us sit at desks all day and are relatively inactive, stretching out becomes more essential to avoid injuries. The key is to strengthen your core, as your abdominal muscles transfer power between your lower and upper body. Experts say that developing strong abs may actually help with back pain by making you less prone to injuries and teaching proper spinal alignment.

Biking is also a great aerobic exercise (if you have the time), as is spinning, which incorporates a combination of light weight training, aerobic stationary biking to piped-in music, and an instructor with a passion for pain. Swimming is less impactful and a good choice for all, especially people with physical limitations. Try to do something that you like to initiate your workout. Make fitness fun. If you hate your workout regimen, you will be less likely to make it a part of your everyday life.

Owning my own business does allow for a bit more flexibility; however, we can all carve out an hour two to three times a week. Simply prioritize. If you can do more, great. Don't think this is the one-hour-a-day-to-a-fit-body-and-life book. The more exercise you do and the healthier your diet, the better. You simply can't out-train a bad diet!

> **"The second day of a diet is always easier than the first. By the second day, you're off it."**
> **—Jackie Gleason**

Remember, this is basic and honest—no sales pitch. There is nothing wrong with joining a gym or getting a personal trainer (if you can afford one). Being surrounded by health-conscious, fit people can help motivate you to reach greater results. Proper instruction is critical, but once you learn, you're ready to fly solo. Something is better than nothing. There is a great line from the U2 song "Miracle Drug":

"There is no failure here, Sweetheart, just when you quit."

If you don't give up, you're in the game. Start slowly and then challenge yourself to increase the increments of weights and the distance and pace of your run. You will be surprised at what you are actually capable of.

No one is telling you to starve yourself, either. Deprivation is not the answer. Just cut out the bread and eat reasonable portions of chicken, sushi, or salads for lunch. Have the veal parmesan with the sautéed spinach instead of linguini. Have a burger if you must, but lose the fries, drink a lot of water, and if you can do without half the bun, great. Try to avoid emotional eating as best you can.

Hydration is key, especially when drinking alcohol—the only problem is getting up every twenty minutes to go the bathroom. Even making a concerted effort to eat healthy can be challenging. Ask for the sauce for your fish on the side, so you can control the distribution, and make sure your side order of veggies isn't finished off with a stick of butter. Mocha frappuccinos with whipped cream and drizzled caramel for your breakfast drink? Not so much! I'm not going to give you a menu—just use good judgment.

I don't eat breakfast myself, just a couple of cups of coffee and occasionally dry cereal or fruit. Yeah, I know, "healthiest meal of the day"—I got it! Actually, new scientific data shows that skipping breakfast enables the body to burn off stored body fat, so take that, you breakfast pushers. It's unrealistic in our busy lives to follow some professional athlete's or movie star's workout and diet regimen. Everyone has his or her own idea of the perfect body. It's not one-size-fits-all.

> **"It's not about looking younger, but looking better."**
> **—Bobby Brown, makeup artist**

Perfection is not the goal; the goal is a comfortable weight and a body type that looks good to you. Unfortunately, your weight is the one place in life where it's easier to gain than to lose. Simply buying flattering cloths that fit your own individual body type can make a difference in your appearance and attitude. With all the different discount and knockoff stores today, you have no excuse. Fashion is affordable for any size or budget.

For most of us, the objective is simply to be the best version of ourselves. The goal is to lose weight (not reach zero body fat), get toned (not ripped), and figure out how to make this part of your everyday lifestyle. The best way to do that is through action (not words), moderation, and logic. Don't put off tomorrow what you can do today.

> **"It's a beautiful day; don't let it get away."**
> **—U2, "Beautiful Day"**

Seize the moment! Set realistic goals and create timetables that are attainable. Don't set yourself up for failure before you begin. Try to reach smaller plateaus and revise your aspirations accordingly. You will be surprised how motivating positive results can be—that's all the reinforcement you will need to inevitably reach your goal. Be true to who and what you want to be.

> **"Find your own truth; it will lead you to the things you love."**
> **—Jax Teller, *Sons of Anarchy***

Don't aspire to the media's definition of what normal and attractive is. You must have your own vision of what success looks like.

"Success leaves clues."
—Lewis Howes, author

By definition, success means a favorable or desired outcome. *Desired* is the key word. We all have our own unique definition of what our desired individual outcome is. What's yours?

Obsessions are unhealthy, and dramatic weight loss or gain can be taxing to the body. Develop healthy habits and choices that you can live with long-term. It makes more sense and is healthier than all these crazy yo-yo diets that have you losing twenty pounds quickly but don't give you the tools to maintain that loss. You end up gaining it all back and damaging your confidence in the process. HBO did a program on obesity titled *The Weight of the Nation* which had a great slogan:

"To Win We Have To Lose"

One of the biggest problems we have is a lack of healthy, cost-conscious options away from home. There are so many fast, fried, fatty food choices smacking us in the face and tempting us to be weak. Brown bagging it is the best option. This way, you can choose exactly what you want. However, it's not always the best social option, so find a few reasonable places close by and go with it.

It's all about choices. We choose to be what we eat. Make healthier choices, and you will see a difference. Stop lying to yourself! Going to a salad bar for lunch sounds good, but these days salad bars serve everything under the sun, hot and cold. Just because you put a little lettuce on your plate doesn't discount the fried wontons, meatballs, and macaroni. (You didn't think anyone was paying attention, did you?) Let logic and moderation dictate your desire.

Another problem is that most people are working harder and longer hours than ever before and are exhausted by the time they get home. It's hard to get up the motivation to work out and easy to fall into bad eating habits, such as eating snacks late in the day.

> **"If we're not meant to have midnight snacks, why is there a light in the fridge?"**
> **—Unknown**

Try taking the stairs instead of the elevator and going out for a long walk at lunchtime. Again, any exercise is good exercise. Drink lots of water (it fills you up, hydrates, and cleanses you) and keep healthy snacks around the house. If your house is filled with unhealthy choices, what choice do you have? If a piece of fruit won't satisfy your hunger, then have a few cookies—just don't have the whole box while dipping them in hot fudge and whipped cream. You get the idea. (Someone out there is laughing. The truth is always funny.) One tip I will give you is this: forget those breakfast muffins that look nuked. I don't care if it is bran (if it is, you better find yourself a potty) or corn or low-fat or low-calorie. Compared to what? The cinnamon bun next to it?

> **"I really don't need buns of steel. I'd be happy with buns of cinnamon."**
> **—Ellen DeGeneres**

You might as well put a candle on it and sing "Happy Birthday" to yourself and forget about the diet, because you just ruined it for the day. But you already knew that, and that's why you're laughing out loud right now. We all lie to ourselves. Just *stop*!

Practice and Preparation

You must be willing to put in the effort to achieve any worthy goal and be the best you can be. A little compulsion and obsession can go a long way toward that dream or goal.

> **"Obsessed is just a word the lazy use to describe the dedicated."**
> **—Russell Warren, author**

Tiger Woods and Michael Jordan were not only the best at what they did, but as documented, they worked the hardest and were the most driven.

> **"I've missed more than nine thousand shots in my career. I've lost almost three hundred games. Twenty-six times, I've been trusted to take the game-winning shot and missed. I've failed over and over and over again in my life. And that is why I succeed."**
> **—Michael Jordan**

> **"The will to win is important, but the will to prepare is vital."**
> **—Joe Paterno, college football coach**

Out-prepare your opponent, and you give yourself the best chance to win. You can approach situations with more confidence, and your experience can give you a mental edge as well.

> **"Failing to prepare is preparing to fail."**
> **—John Wooden, UCLA basketball coach**

It's not enough to have talent or a gift—it's how hard you work to enhance your God-given talents that makes the difference. The separation is in the preparation.

> **"Hard work beats talent when talent doesn't work hard."**
> **—Kevin Durant, NBA basketball player**

How you prepare and practice is equally important. If you just go through the motions, you can't expect to improve. Challenge yourself and be willing to experiment. Prepare for every potential eventuality.

> **"Practice without improvement is meaningless."**
> **—Chuck Knox, NFL football coach**

There will be many moments in your life where you feel outmatched. You can potentially alter the outcome with extra effort and a solid work ethic. Hard work and extra preparation can compensate for a lot.

> **"If you can't outplay them outwork them."**
> **—Ben Hogan, professional golfer**

Work hard and take pride in what you do. Don't be lazy. This thought process also translates to your business and personal life. Take e-mails, for example. I receive so many work e-mails that are written poorly, not spell-checked, and slapped together with minimal thought. I can't understand why someone wouldn't take the extra time to assure that their thoughts are represented with care. That lazy thinking and careless attitude usually reflects other parts of that person's personality and self-image.

If you're instant-messaging a friend, I understand the need for all these crazy abbreviations. (I don't understand most of them, however.) But if you're constructing a business e-mail, use proper English and write like an intelligent person. (We all have spell-check.) If you are sending me a personal e-mail, please don't copy me on all of your spur-of-the-moment thoughts, and don't get me tangled up in a reply-all web of useless responses from people I either don't know or don't care about. We all have a unique opportunity in this Information Age to use technological tools to our advantage. Pay attention to digital etiquette. Don't be lazy—just don't!

Success

Success can be defined as the achievement of something desired, planned, or attempted. For some its prosperity, for others, its fame. Most successful people attribute their success to hard work. I think it has more to do with attitude. You must believe in yourself and have the confidence to chase your dream. Having a positive outlook can help overcome potential obstacles and discouragement. You need to program your mind to be positive, to potentially alter your outcome. Sheer passion, discipline and determination can mean the difference between success and failure and I believe you can't have one without the other.

> **"If you want to increase your success rate, double your failure rate."**
> **—Tom Watson, professional golfer**

No one I know has ever succeeded without trial and error. You need to remain positive when times get tough.

> **"Success is going from failure to failure without losing your enthusiasm."**
> **—Winston Churchill**

Success is a state of mind, and each of us has our own definition as it relates to our own lives. You need to believe that you can do whatever it takes to achieve your desired outcome. People should spend more time chasing a passion and less time chasing money.

"Success usually comes to those who are too busy to be looking for it."
—Henry David Thoreau, poet

Most people who have achieved a level of success have endured much sacrifice. For many, the true measure of success is happiness. Unfortunately, the two don't always coincide. To achieve either, I believe you must first define what they mean to you.

"Success?, I don't know what that word means. I'm happy. But success, that goes back to what in somebody's eyes success means. For me, success is inner peace. That's a good day for me."
—Denzel Washington, actor

The pursuit of success also comes with considerable trade-offs. You have to be willing to sacrifice something at the expense of your end goal. Addressing these trade-offs can be tricky. Prioritize what is most important and what you are willing to compromise. There are no universal answers to what makes sense. It comes down to what makes sense to you at a certain stage of your life. Set your parameters carefully and be honest with yourself as it relates to associated risks and benefits. The pursuit of success is a natural human instinct that we all desire in one form or another. Define success in your own terms and work hard to achieve your goals. We live in a new world filled with instant gratification. Achieving your goals has more to do with hard work, patience and persistence. As I stated earlier, the new generation has an expectation of things going to plan. Sustainability is harder to achieve which is why it's so coveted. Lasting relationships or esteem businesses take time, patience and persistence. Be willing to adjust your strategy toward your goals as you go along. Sometimes, deciding not to pursue certain goals can be just as important to eventual happiness and success. Define what will make you happy and be willing to fight for it. Get going!

"Death and Life"

THAT'S RIGHT; I SAID, "DEATH and life." Most people are so focused on the inevitable end that they lose perspective. Embrace the life you have. Ever notice how no one likes to talk about it? As if not speaking about it will increase your life expectancy? Look, death sucks—unless you think something greater is waiting on the other side.

"I'm not afraid of death; I just don't want to be there when it happens."
—Woody Allen

Yogi Berra's wife asked, "Yogi, when you die, where do you want to be buried? In Montclair, New York, or in St. Louis?" Yogi replied, "I don't know, Carmen, why don't you surprise me?"

Religious belief can be comforting, and there's always the potential fountain of youth for the optimistic crowd. Cryogenics could work—you never know what cures they will come up with, although I'm not really sure I want to be around that far in the future, hanging out with Walt Disney and the head of Ted Williams. So my approach is to work hard, be responsible, live life for today, take good care of myself, enjoy a few vices, and hope for a bit of luck! Take control and live your life.

"Every man dies. Not every man really lives."
—William Wallace, *Braveheart*

Being alive is not the same as living. Life is a gift, no matter what your view of the hereafter. Cherish it, enjoy it, and if you are fortunate enough to believe in the afterlife, that's a bonus for you.

"You only live once, but if you do it right, once is enough."
—Mae West, actress

Treat others as you would hope to be treated, and be willing to laugh at yourself. Perfection is overrated and doesn't seem like that much fun to me. Embrace your imperfections and dysfunctions and understand that you are not alone. Don't spend your whole life searching for answers; instead, define the person you want to be.

"Life isn't about finding yourself. Life is about creating yourself."
—George Bernard Shaw, Irish playwright

We are all a little dysfunctional; the question is, to what degree? Limit it before being consumed by it. Make an effort to evolve with age and learn from your mistakes. We all wish we knew then, what we know now.

"Life can only be understood backwards; but it must be lived forwards."
—Soren Kierkegard, Danish philosopher

Be willing to listen to others and find a passion. The idea of dying is truly scary, but don't allow the fear to consume. Instead, let it motivate you to really live.

"I'm not afraid of dying. I'm afraid of not trying."
—Jay-Z, "Beach Chair"

We are all so caught up in equating success with possessions and financial gain that we tend to lose sight of what's really important. A man's worth should be measured by the size of his heart, not the size of his bank account. Don't confuse wealth with success. What did a person give back, and who did they touch along the way? I recently lost my father-in-law (Poppy) to cancer, and his grandkids delivered a poignant poem at his service that captured his true essence. He was a sweet and gentle, intelligent man from a different generation, of simple means. He was unassuming, consistent, and left a profound and lasting impression. I said in a eulogy at his funeral that in the thirty-plus years that I knew him, I did not have one negative memory of him—how many people can you say that about? Here is the poem:

> **What Is the Measure of a Man?**
> **Not *How did he die?* But *How did he live?***
> **Not *What did he gain?* But *What did he give?***
> **These are the units to measure the worth**
> **Of a man as a man, regardless of birth.**
> **Not *What was his station?* But *Had he a heart?***
> **And *How did he play his lifelong part?***
> ***Was he ever ready with a word of good cheer?***
> ***To bring back a smile, to banish a tear?***
> **Not *What was his shrine?* Nor *What was his creed?***

But *Had he befriended those really in need*
Not *What did the sketch in the newspaper say?*
But *How many were sorry when he passed away?*

Don't let life get in the way of living. Do things while you're here that make you happy. Life will happen; it's your choice how you live it.

> **"Life should not be a journey to the grave with the intention of arriving safely in a pretty and well-preserved body, but rather to skid in broadside in a cloud of smoke, thoroughly used up, totally worn out, and loudly proclaiming 'Wow, what a ride!'"**
> **—Hunter S. Thompson, author**

It's not about what you take with you; it's about what you leave behind. Leave a legacy of love and cherished memories that you can pass on to your children and grandchildren. Make life happen!

> **"The best dreams happen when you're awake."**
> **—Cherie Gilderbloom, author**

Life is like a story, with a beginning, a middle, and an end. What's the story you're leaving behind?

> **"Don't cry because it's over. Smile because it happened."**
> **—Dr. Seuss**

Be a good person and try to discover happiness in your life. Richard Branson, best known as the founder and chairman of Virgin Group, said:

"The best measure of success is happiness."

Seems like a pretty happy guy to me! My son's favorite quote of all time is from John Lennon:

> **"When I was five years old, my mother always told me that happiness was the key to life. When I went to school, they asked me what I wanted to be when I grew up. I wrote down 'happy.' They told me I didn't understand the assignment, and I told them they didn't understand life."**

We all have the ability to be happy. For some, it's a choice; for others, it's a way of life. Either way, it's well worth the effort. Be kind to others and live a life in peace. As John Lennon wrote in his song "Imagine":

> **"Imagine all the people**
> **Living life in peace …**
> **You may say I'm a dreamer**
> **But I'm not the only one**
> **I hope someday you'll join us**
> **And the world will be as one."**

The funny thing is that the longer I live, the worse my eyesight gets, yet, the more vivid and beautiful life becomes. Can't wait for the next chapter. I'm just glad I survived this far!

> **"What a long, strange trip it's been.**
> **—Grateful Dead, "Truckin'"**

"Quote Me"

Plastic Surgery

If it makes you feel good, then "just do it"! Again, moderation is important. See *Plastic Surgery Gone Wild*—you get the point. I think you should be at least seventeen to decide for yourself. Don't let other people tell you what looks good or is good for you. Usually those people just don't have the guts to do it. Not that I'm advocating changing your appearance, but if a nip or tuck or a bit of botulism makes you feel better about yourself, then go for it, babe! Just as in drinking, do it responsibly, and realize that less is more! Do your research! News flash: there are good and bad doctors, not one-size-fits-all! Here, the best-price theory does not apply. You are going to have to look at that mistake in the mirror every day for the rest of your life, so do your homework. You could always go the other route like me and convince yourself that your Roman nose adds character.

Charity

Charity is important, and we should all give what we can, whether monetarily or through effort and involvement. Giving back feels good, but just stop making me feel bad because I don't have the time, patience, or money for every telemarketer collecting for one of a million charities. We each have those charities that are dear to us, and none of us is Bill Gates, so back off and stop making me feel like shit because you walked around the block for herpes. Not interested!

Disclaimers

Is it me, or has the world gone mad? Don't you love these ads for one pill or the other helping this problem or that, and at the end of the ad, they state that it could or may cause a laundry list of other more dire ailments way worse than the one you started with? Granted, you will certainly forget about your headache when you discover that you have anal leakage and need to investigate adult diapers.

Racism/Bigotry/Discrimination

Bad! Bad! Bad! Who cares what color, religion, or sexual orientation people are as long as they can coexist in a nonextreme fashion? Why should someone's sexual orientation matter to you? As if that orientation will rub off. My feeling is that you are or you aren't, and why are we still discussing this in the twenty-first century anyway? As Maya Angelou professed, "We are more alike, my friends, than we are unalike." In the words of Rodney King, "Why can't we all just get along?" It seems simple enough. This proves my theory that you can learn something from anyone. You just have to listen!

Sweet Dreams

Altering your consciousness can alter your subconscious. Attitude and approach can alter the way you view things. Choose your mood. Condition yourself to go to bed with positive, happy thoughts, and you will wake up well rested. Watch *Seinfeld* or *Fallon* instead of *The Walking Dead* before you turn out the lights. If you're stressing about work, think of a few proactive ideas to start with the next day. For example, if you are in danger of being downsized at work, don't wait for the ax to fall. Update your résumé and find ways to be less dispensable by being proactive rather than reactive. Well, either that, or a couple of Ambien should do the trick.

Judging

Too many people today are so quick to judge others without real knowledge or information. Things are not always what they seem. Life is difficult, and we all have our own way of dealing with things. Your way is not necessarily the right way. It's simply the right way for you. Keep an open mind and be willing to accept and embrace differences. Be flexible and open-minded and give people the benefit of the doubt. Don't believe everything you hear, and don't be so quick to judge people. *Just don't!*

The Grass Is Always Greener
It's not!

Sports

I love 'em all. What else could bring ten homophobic male strangers together to ass-slap and hug each other while getting inebriated at any given bar?

Money Can't Buy Happiness

I thought we were being honest.

Service Men and Women

Let me be perfectly clear: I don't care about your political point of view! Any time you see a man or woman in uniform, *thank them* and/or *hug them*! They are protecting our freedom with their lives!

Less Is More

We have become a diet/vitamin/antidepressant pharmaceutical society of overindulgence. If you are going to partake, then see a nutritionist or physician before you do a self-diagnosis. Side effects and safety risks should be addressed. Everyone's chemical and physical makeup is unique, and self-prescribing more than the recommended amount of medication or supplements can have adverse effects. The term *natural* is not necessarily a synonym for *safe*. Bottom line: less is more!

Music

It sets the mood, calms the soul, revs you up, brings you down, brings people together, inspires, brings you to your knees, makes you move, and provides a soundtrack to your life. Music reflects the culture, marks time through poetic verse, and allows for free expression and an individual sense of style. Top that!

People

Love all shapes, sizes, colors, creeds, and ages. Love people with confidence and an inner beauty. Beauty is indeed "in the eye of the beholder." Be willing to "behold" and look beneath the surface. Just try it!

Guns

How many massacres will we have to endure before we have a serious conversation regarding gun control? We need to remove the killing machines and high-capacity ammunition clips from the streets. No one is saying it will completely eliminate these senseless acts, but it will markedly reduce the events. The Second Amendment was enacted in 1791, when the weapon of choice was a musket, not an AK-47. I'm all good with the right to defend yourself with a firearm (legally), although I choose not to. But we are in different times, and the spirit of the amendment is far outdated. The NRA stands for National Rifle Association; hunting rifles are not the concern here, so let's stop using the "right to bear arms" as an excuse for assault weapons invading our culture. The original intent of the amendment was to defend communities against massacres, not as a means to enable such massacres. If the brutal killing of twenty first-graders in Newtown, Connecticut, is not the last straw in this conversation, then we have much bigger problems. It's our obligation to protect our children. I am all good with natural disasters, having recently endured Hurricane Sandy, but Newtown is unnatural in every way and just may be avoidable. I don't pretend to have the answers, but let sensibility override other agendas. Let's honor these children and their families with change. This is not about right or left; it's simply about right or wrong!

The Good News Network

I wish there was a "Positive Only" News Network where they highlighted all the good in the world that goes unreported. We have become an over sensationalized, train-wreck-reporting, TMZ society of intrusive paparazzi and irresponsible media. Why do we have to endure so many negative stories per day in a world that I truly believe is innately filled with good? The Sunday morning news with Charles Osgood (recently retired) is a unique and refreshing example of how the news can be a positive experience. Why can't the good stories that inspire win the day over the stories that perpetuate fear and depravity? Let's call it the "Good News Network"! Sounds like a job for Richard Branson.

About the Author

Steven Pollack graduated from Stony Brook University in 1983 with a bachelor's degree in psychology. He founded his company, Pollack Resource Management, Inc., an executive search firm based in Manhattan, in 1990. Steven has been married for more than twenty-five years and has two children. He was born and still resides in New York City on the North Shore of Long Island. This is his first book and a labor of love.

To learn more about Steven, you can visit him at:

www.stevenpollackbooks.com
@stevenpollack88

As this book is a life in progress, I reserve the right for further editions.

Printed in the United States
By Bookmasters